I0446221

GET CLEAR ON AI

HOW AI IS SHAPING YOUR JOB, YOUR BUSINESS, AND OUR GLOBAL FUTURE

JON MORRISON

Copyright © 2023 by Jon Morrison

ISBN: 9798865671091

All rights reserved.

No part of this book may be reproduced in any form or by any electronic or mechanical means, including information storage and retrieval systems, without written permission from the author, except for the use of brief quotations in a book review.

CONTENTS

Preface: How I Wrote A Book About AI With The Help
Of AI   v
Introduction   ix

PART ONE

AI BASICS

1. What AI Can Do And Will Do   3
2. What Is AI Really?   13
3. AI-Related Terms You Need to Know   22

PART TWO

AI INTEGRATION AND MANAGING CHANGE

4. Overcoming AI Implementation Hurdles   35
5. Values Are The Foundation of AI Integration   41
6. Choosing the Right AI Tools   55
7. Customer-Oriented AI   58
8. How You'll Adapt Your Business to AI   65
9. Crushing it with Content   71
10. Managing Change with Your Team   80

PART THREE

ETHICAL AI USE

When Progress Brings Up the Challenges of Power and
Responsibility   93
11. Navigating Through the Ethical Age of AI   95
12. Navigating Your Policy Decisions   104
13. Risks and Transparency   109
14. How I Wrote a Book with the Help of AI   113
15. Embracing Ethical Writing in the Age of AI   114

Conclusion: Just Scratching the Surface of AI Ethics   119
Finale - Looking Down the Path While Standing at a
Crossroads   121
About Jon Morrison   133
Acknowledgments   137

PREFACE: HOW I WROTE A BOOK ABOUT AI WITH THE HELP OF AI

Look at that. You're still reading a book. That's amazing.

Books have been our companions for thousands of years. AI seems to be the latest thing. But it's not really all that new. There's a saying that 'the fish will be the last to see the water.' In our context, AI is like the water and we are the fish. The water is so essential to our environment that we often fail to notice its presence until we're forced to. I write to help us both 'see the water,' to recognize and understand the ubiquitous yet often invisible force of AI that surrounds us.

It's as if we awoke one day to find AI everywhere, influencing every aspect of our lives. I felt like I needed to learn everything in 2x speed just to keep pace with all that was coming out. Honestly, two years ago, I'd be more competent to write a book about A1, the BBQ sauce, than AI, artificial intelligence.

Having written several books already, I wanted to see how AI could help this time. I started with ChatGPT, the darling and first love of AI enthusiasts like me. "I am going to write a book," I typed, "focused on AI, with a focus on small business owners looking to understand what it is and how it could help them. What might this look like as an outline?"

In return, ChatGPT offered a framework, a starting point from which this exploration of AI could begin.

"Truly amazing," I thought to myself. It used to be that the draft of book outlines took months, maybe even years to create.

My prompt and output was the catalyst I needed to get things started.

While that first outline was helpful, now that I'm done with the book, I notice that I used very few of those early ideas.

However, those early moments were highly beneficial to get me started.

After some thinking, I soon had my own, AI-inspired outline for a book. I write books on Google Doc. Nothing fancy there. I started filling it with thoughts, rough notes, half-baked ideas, and some stories and statistics I have been collecting. Most writers say that this is one of the most fun stages in book writing. You're not even writing. You're only researching, learning, thinking, praying, listening to podcasts, signing up for every webinar, subscribing to far too many newsletters, and slowly discovering what you really believe about a subject.

That, to me, is the great joy of writing - it's the learning.

And then, to do justice to all that learning, I have to write it all out. Or hire a ghostwriter (which more authors do than you ever thought).

At least that's the way it used to happen. There is now amazing news for those of us who love to write but hate to write as well.

Let Me Tell You How I Wrote This Book

Once I had done enough research to feel like I had something of value to offer, I asked ChatGPT to take my notes and turn them into prose. I read through every output. They were pretty good. I read through and then double-checked it all to ensure authenticity and originality. As a lifelong student, I didn't want to be plagiarizing. I ran the text through my plagiarism checker Grammarly (which also uses AI), and everything came out 100% unique. Amazing!

Working through the book's content, I noticed a subtle dance of give and take with the AI. I provided the strategy, and ChatGPT offered the heavy lifting of writing text that sounded like me. This took time. There was a lot of "No, try again...try again, this time do _____..."
Once I had a manuscript I liked, I sent it to a wonderful human, my editor, Justin Chevrier, who went through it all. He sent it back with a whole bunch of improvements. Eventually, I got to a point where I was delighted to provide holding in your hands now.

While AI certainly helped me get my work done quicker, I can assure you that the positions held are mine. The recommendations are from me. But the credit for getting it all together within a mind-blowing timeframe (a new personal best record time for book writing at three months) belongs to artificial intelligence.

I find encouragement from a quote attributed to Mary Shelley, the author of "Frankenstein." It goes: "It is better to write a book quickly than to spend too long on it." Shelley's writing process for a her classic work, "Frankenstein" was apparently quick and she believed that was the best way to publish a book.

Like you, I have ongoing questions and concerns about AI (as I do with all technology). But I absolutely love how AI has helped me here. I also love the reaction I get when I show people what AI can do for them too. Their production and creativity skyrockets. That's why I know a book like this will help so many others.

As it has helped us, I know it will help you.

We Still Need Humanity

Maybe I'm still an old-school writer because human touch is still paramount to me. Each word, paragraph, and chapter was sifted through a fine mesh of scrutiny, ensuring my voice – human, grounded, and genuine – was not lost amidst the AI's proficient outputs.

The result of this intricate interplay between technology and human creativity was *Get Clear On AI*, a book that, from cover to cover, represents a journey through the new yet fascinating world of artificial intelligence.

And so, as you work through these pages, remember: this is not just a how-to guide about AI but also a case study of what happens when human curiosity meets machine efficiency.

I hope this work, born from the intertwining of technology and human experience, empowers and enlightens your journey of understanding what AI is and how it can help your business.

Perhaps this book is *YOUR* catalyst to finally getting the book done that you've always wanted to write.

If I can do it, I know you certainly can, too! I hope you enjoy this one.

Sincerely,

INTRODUCTION

As the clock ticks towards 2:30 pm in another afternoon that has gone by too fast, I close my laptop to wrap up the workday.

I take off my "Small Business Owner" hat and put on my "Dad" hat. 2:30 is the time to join my wife on our weekday routine to pick up the kids from school. It's also a time to connect with the other dads who work from home before we collectively head into the chaos of being a parent in the 21st century. Soon, I will put another hat on labelled "Coach." I'm not just a father to three wonderful daughters but also their ice hockey coach. Due to my wife and I's "2 years apart" family planning, the girls are staggered in age, so they will always play on different teams. As you can imagine, many afternoons or evenings are spent at rinks around British Columbia's Fraser Valley. It's on the ice that I do my best to pass on the joys of hockey to the next generation. It's a sport that's been a significant part of my life and has given me so much. I find it very meaningful to give back.

Balancing my role as a coach with my professional commitments requires hard work and efficiency. Working from home, I've learned to maximize my productivity in my limited hours before parenting or coaching duties call.

And that's why I love AI. It helps me do better at the things I value.

Artificial Intelligence has emerged as a quiet yet powerful force in this constant juggling of responsibilities. It's streamlined my work processes, allowing me to accomplish more in less time. I write faster, I think quicker. My creative output has doubled. AI isn't just about sophisticated technology; it's about practical solutions that make our daily work more efficient. It has become an indispensable part of my work life, aiding me in serving my clients effectively despite my shortened workday.

This is an invitation for you to explore the practicalities of AI for those who are wearing many hats, running small businesses and managing tight schedules.

It's about understanding how AI can be a tool for better use of our time, enhanced productivity, and a more rewarding life. It's a story of how technology can be harnessed to serve our needs, helping us better professionals, parents, and even coaches, if that's your thing.

Every day, artificial intelligence is reshaping industries at an unprecedented speed.

It creates new winners and losers at a breathtaking pace. Businesses that ignore its impact risk becoming obsolete.

Those who embrace it can unlock unprecedented opportunities. If the thought of being left behind in the rapidly evolving world of AI keeps you up at night, you're not alone. Many business owners feel the same.

WHY "GET CLEAR ON AI"?

This is your guide to understanding and harnessing the power of AI in life and business. I'm writing to publish something for the person who knows nothing about AI but is curious about what it could do for them. I cut through the jargon, delivering clear and actionable insights tailored for small business owners like you.

I'm going to unravel the complexities of AI, transforming intricate concepts into simple, actionable strategies that any business owner can grasp. As you go move through the pages you'll explore real-world applications, gaining insights into how AI directly impacts your industry and the numerous ways you can harness its power to your advantage.

But it's not just about the what and the how; the ethics surrounding AI usage are also crucial. This book offers a guiding hand through the waters of AI ethics. I want to ensure that as you advance, your business stays grounded and on the right path. "Get Clear On AI" equips you with future-proof strategies to stay ahead. These insights and techniques will not only help you adapt but also stay ahead, ensuring you remain relevant in the coming years.

THE DIFFERENCE AI WILL MAKE

As a small business owner, you may wonder whether AI is worth the hype. Can it genuinely make a difference in your business? As evidenced by a groundbreaking study conducted by Boston Consulting Group and top social scientists, the answer is a resounding YES.[1]

A comprehensive experiment with consultants showed that those using AI, specifically the ChatGPT-4 model, consistently outperformed their peers who didn't use AI. Here's a breakdown of the impressive results from those who used AI at work:

- *12.2% more tasks completed:* Imagine the advantage of processing over a tenth more customer requests or completing additional projects in the same time.
- *Tasks were completed 25.1% faster:* Speed is of the essence in business, and with AI, you can respond to market changes and customer needs significantly faster.
- *40% higher quality results:* Delivering top-notch products or services is a priority for every business. AI can help ensure that your output isn't just faster but also of superior quality.[2]

That could be your results too. What would you do if you were 10% more effective, 25% faster and doing 40% better work?

I'm writing to empower small business owners to leverage AI technology to its fullest potential and maintain a high standard of ethical practices by giving them the tools and knowledge they need to navigate societal changes and keep up with the ever-shifting business landscape.

Before we get to all the benefits, let's figure out what people mean when they talk about AI.

GETTING OUR HEADS AROUND AI

The pace of technology adoption has been breathtaking in recent decades. Historically, the telephone took 75 years to reach 100 million users, while the mobile phone achieved this feat in 16 years. Adopting the Internet to 100 million took 7 years, with social platforms like Facebook and Instagram taking only 4.5 and 2.5 years to reach that many users. The rapid rise of TikTok surprised many, reaching 100 million users in only 9 months. The AI innovation, ChatGPT, smashed this record, reaching the same number of users in an astonishing *2 months*! This accelerated adoption underscores the immense value and potential users see in AI-driven technologies, bringing in a new era in tech adoption rates[3].

Though people are opening accounts and playing around with how ChatGPT creates a tasty gluten-free muffin recipe, small business owners need to take advantage of its potential in their businesses.

Despite AI's promising opportunities, its adoption among small businesses could be faster. The McKinsey Global Institute projects that by 2025, AI could contribute up to $13 trillion of value across various sectors, equating to an additional 1.2% annual GDP growth.[4]

THE POWER OF AI IS UNDENIABLE

AI is a transformative force reshaping how businesses operate and deliver value. From enhancing customer interactions to streamlining complex tasks, AI's capabilities are ushering in a new era of efficiency and innovation.

The following results underscore AI's profound impact on various professional domains, highlighting its potential to drive significant productivity gains. Consider these results from another study:

- Support agents using AI handled 13.8% more customer inquiries per hour.
- Business professionals using AI wrote 59% more business documents per hour.
- Programmers using AI coded 126% more projects per week.[5]

Across all industries worldwide, AI is improving how regular people like you and I get work done.

BUT NOT EVERYONE IS USING IT

Data from the SMB Group reveals that as of 2021, 70% of small businesses still need to integrate even the basic AI tools into their operations. [6]

This juxtaposition is telling: while AI offers transformative potential, a significant segment of the small business community has yet to embrace this technology. The prospects for innovation, efficiency, and competitive advantage are substantial for those who decide to step into AI.

It might not have affected you *yet*, but it will. AI is changing everything.

From recommendations on what to watch to personalized advertisements on what to buy, AI-powered systems are constantly making predictions and providing us with information, all of which help us in our daily lives.

Although some may still be wary of this technology, it's already clear that AI is all around us and, in many ways, is permanently intertwined with modern society. This is especially true in the business world, where we will focus our attention throughout this book.

This new and largely unexplored technology will revolutionize how we do things in every field. Jobs will be created. Jobs will be lost. You can expect a steady stream of new "game-changing" products and services.

As AI continues to grow and evolve rapidly, business owners must understand how to use it effectively and ethically.

This book discusses the opportunities and challenges of integrating AI and how we can implement it ethically and responsibly to benefit our businesses and customers.

Readers will learn about AI terminology, implementation strategies, and ethical considerations for building a successful AI-driven business.

THE DAY EVERYTHING CHANGED FOR ME

I've told you about why I use AI. Let me back up to when I made the decision that I would leverage its power rather than be crushed by it.

When I started the entrepreneurship journey in 2016, I had a clear vision of how I wanted to run my business: *to fuel the growth of small businesses reach more customers with outstanding marketing.* I was hired to be a company's wordsmith, crafting compelling narratives for their pitches, websites, and email campaigns. I helped guide companies in narrating their unique stories. If there was something I was called on to do that was beyond my skills, I had a trusty network of contractors I could rely on to help.

As time passed, in 2022, I met a new best friend in business: *artificial intelligence.*

I didn't know how it worked. I just saw that it worked. Figuring out the how of AI was something I'd take on another day. In the meantime, during those thrilling early AI adoption days, it was like unlocking a secret door in my craft. It saved me so many hours.

With AI, I could write faster, think quicker, and create captivating content on a scale I had never imagined. The need for additional contractors reduced dramatically as I could generate bountiful content in mere minutes. This kept profits in my company, allowed me to reinvest in my own development (taking courses on AI) and feeding my family.

I fell in love with AI. The more I learned, the more I saw its potential.

However, in those days, I discovered that using it in business was not something people discussed openly. Early adopters only discussed AI in hushed voices within the security of quiet, dimly lit rooms. We knew the disruption it would cause in our industry if word got out.

Then one day, in November 2022, the word got out.

OpenAI released ChatGPT to the public.

It was one of those days in history where everything changed. My secret was discovered.

REINVENTION

This new application enabled everyone to tap into the power of AI technology.

Suddenly, my unique selling point didn't seem so unique. Services I used to charge thousands of dollars were available in just a few minutes through a free AI application.

Our once steady stream of content writing requests began to dry up. The AI tools could do it all. The word was spreading through the marketplace and society. What was once a marketers' best-kept secret was now the conversation topic among the other dads at my kids' school pickup.

My industry was disrupted. The secret was all over the news. As AI took over content generation tasks, I found fewer people asking for help with writing. I had to adapt to the new realities of the marketplace or watch my business die.

Instead of declaring war on AI like so many have done, I decided to join forces with it.

I reinvented my role, morphing from a marketing consultant into an AI guide for small business owners. I had my developer create an AI tool we could offer our clients. It was a brand message generator (brandmessage.ai). It could do what used to take me days in under a minute. We used to charge $1500 for this service. Now, AI is doing it for free. Then we developed the next step, taking that AI-generated message and turning it into an elevator pitch and the outline (plus words) of an entire website. With AI, it was all done now in minutes for almost no cost.

That's disruption.

No problem. I believe what's good for the clients is good for the agency.

My mission shifted from doing the writing for small businesses to teaching them how to leverage AI in their operations. I started teaching people how to wield AI tools effectively, helping them navigate this brave new world with opportunistic courage.

The journey has been incredible. I've watched businesses transform their operations, save time, create content, reach new people, and grow their brands.

And the best part? I'm at the heart of this transformation, helping shape a future where humans and machines collaborate to create extraordinary outcomes.

Every day brings fresh challenges, novel insights, and the chance to impact businesses positively.

WHAT AI WILL DO FOR OUR JOBS

With every new chapter, a looming question casts a shadow on the technological marvel of AI: What does this mean for our jobs? Are we on the brink of a world where machines take over the roles we've held dear for all these years?

As we stand at this crossroads, addressing the elephant in the room is essential: *Will the rise of AI script an end to significant job roles, or is there another twist in the tale?*

Let's look at the sensitive topic of AI and its impact on jobs.

THE ALARMING STATS FROM MCKINSEY

During the pandemic from 2019 to 2022, the U.S. labor market experienced a significant shift, with 8.6 million occupational changes, 50% more than the previous three years. Most of these shifts involved individuals transitioning from sectors like food services, in-person sales, and office support. Looking ahead to 2030, it's projected that as much as 30% of the work hours currently being done in the U.S. economy could become automated, a trend that generative AI is likely to accelerate.[7]

Here's my point: Our workplace is shifting already, and it's only going to increase.

HISTORICAL PERSPECTIVE: TECHNOLOGY AND JOB DISPLACEMENT

As we journey through the annals of history, we find that our current predicament isn't entirely new. Think back to the Industrial Revolution, when steam-powered machines began to hum and whir, taking over tasks that were once done by human hands. There was a collective gasp, a fear that these machines would replace the workforce. And then came the computers, those magical boxes that promised efficiency but also stirred worries about job losses. Sound familiar?

But here's the twist in our story: With each technological leap, society didn't just stand still; it adapted, grew, and evolved. New roles emerged, economies shifted, and we found ways to coexist with these innovations.

Consider the agricultural revolution, a precursor to the industrial age. Centuries ago, a vast majority of the population (estimates suggest over 90%) was engaged in food production. The advent of agricultural technologies significantly reduced the number of people needed for farming, leading to a dramatic decrease in the percentage of the population involved in food production. This shift was monumental. It didn't just change how we grew food; it freed up human resources, allowing more people to engage in other pursuits that propelled civilization forward – in arts, science, education, and industry.

The lessons from our past are clear. While technology has the power to displace, it also has the incredible ability to create, innovate, and open doors we never knew existed. As we take on AI and all its opportunities and challenges, it's worth remembering that this isn't our first rodeo. We've been here, we've faced change, and we've always found a way to write a new chapter. The transition from agriculture to industrial and now to the digital age shows us that, as one door closes, another opens, often leading to paths of greater progress and prosperity.

WHAT'S GREAT FOR YOUR BUSINESS OFTEN COMES AT A COST

With the help of AI, tasks are executed with unparalleled efficiency, decisions are better, and businesses can operate leaner and more profitably than ever before.

However, with this transformation comes a real human element for which I have the utmost compassion. The integration of AI might mean that some roles within the company will evolve or, in some cases, become redundant. It's a tough reality for both the business owner and the employee. But it's essential to remember that every technological advancement has shifted the job market. The key lies in adaptation and resilience.

For the proactive business owner who loves their employees (and most that I've met do), this is an opportunity to retrain and upskill their team. Employees can be transitioned into roles requiring a human touch, which AI can't replicate. Whether in creative thinking, relationship-building, or strategy formulation, there's a vast array of areas where human expertise will always be irreplaceable.

For those employees facing the reality of their roles changing, this period represents a crossroads. It's a chance to embrace new learning, pivot, and find a path that aligns with the future. The world is changing, but with change comes opportunity. It's a moment to rediscover passions, learn new skills, and step into roles that might be more fulfilling and aligned with the future of work.

THE AI SOLUTION IN A CONTRADICTORY ECONOMY

A peculiar paradox presents itself in the current economic landscape. On the one hand, we're living in one of the most challenging economic climates in recent history. Yet, on the other hand, unemployment rates remain surprisingly low. "Help Wanted" signs hang everywhere you turn in windows, and online job boards are flooded with openings. Business owners, from small startups to established corporations, voice a common concern: a dwindling interest in entry-level positions.

It's a problem that has left many puzzled: *Why is there a disinterest in available jobs in a struggling economy?* Some speculate it's a generational shift in work values, while others believe it's a quest for better work-life balance or a desire for roles that offer immediate upward mobility.

AI is the unexpected solution to this modern-day challenge. Artificial intelligence doesn't aspire for the lowest amount of energy output. It doesn't seek work-life balance, nor does it advocate for the three-day workweek. It's always available to take on those currently overlooked entry-level roles.

To me, this is the silver lining for business owners in a complex economic cloud. AI offers a reliable, cost-effective solution to the hiring challenges they face. It can fill the gaps, ensuring that businesses run smoothly and customers continue receiving the expected services.

It's essential to approach this transition with sensitivity and foresight. While AI can undoubtedly handle many entry-level tasks, the human touch remains irreplaceable in various aspects of business. As we integrate AI into the workforce, we must ensure that human employees are given opportunities to upskill, innovate, and take on roles that require empathy, creativity, and human judgment.

In essence, the rise of AI in this contradictory economy isn't a replacement of the human workforce but a reshaping of it. It's an evolution that, if approached wisely, can lead to a more efficient, innovative, and harmonious business landscape.

BRIDGING THE WORKFORCE GAP: AI'S ROLE IN A CHANGING DEMOGRAPHIC LANDSCAPE

For years, economists and business leaders have cast a wary eye on the shifting demographics of our workforce. The baby boomer generation, one of the largest and most influential in history, is steadily moving into retirement. Coupled with a declining birth rate, this has sparked concerns about a potential workforce vacuum. The looming question has been: Who will fill the shoes of these retiring professionals? How will industries sustain themselves with a shrinking pool of young talent?

This demographic challenge is now being viewed in a new light, thanks to the advancements in AI. Technology might solve another one of our workforce problems.

Instead of viewing the retiring baby boomers as a loss, we can see this transition as a chance to reshape and redefine industries' operations.

This doesn't mean human roles become obsolete; instead, the nature of jobs will evolve. The workforce of the future will likely be a blend of humans and AI, working in tandem. Humans will take on more specialized roles, focusing on tasks that require emotional intelligence, creativity, and complex problem-solving.

THE SMALL BUSINESS OWNER'S GUIDE TO LEVERAGING THE POWER OF AI

If you're reading this book and want to learn about AI as quickly as possible, you'll appreciate my journey. You're a business owner intrigued by artificial intelligence, but unsure how it can benefit your business. You also want to ensure you're not part of the problem. The last thing any of us want is to confess to our grandkids that we accidentally programmed the robotic dog to "byte" the mailman instead of the ball.

This silly scenario highlights a serious point: the importance of thoughtful and ethical programming in AI. We want to use AI, but we want to do it right – ensuring our technological advances are beneficial, not just amusing missteps.

Together, I believe we can still navigate this world of AI, keeping both its immense potential and our responsibility in mind.

You want to use AI, but you also want to do it the right way.

Me too.

Whether you're a small business owner or an established small business owner looking to stay ahead of the curve, you'll receive timely insights and strategies for incorporating AI into your work.

I take a practical approach to demystifying the complexity of AI and making it accessible to all business owners.

Soon you'll get a working definition of AI and a breakdown of the different types of AI to ensure that even those who have never interacted with AI can understand it. I aim to empower business owners with the knowledge to make informed decisions about incorporating AI into their business operations.

I will teach you how to leverage AI technology to improve your business processes, and you will also gain insights into the ethical considerations surrounding AI usage.

Before we do that, however, we need to deal with some of the baggage you might be bringing into the discussion.

ARE FICTIONAL SCI-FI THRILLERS BECOMING REAL-LIFE POSSIBILITIES?

Movies have been some of the most influential elements in shaping the public perception of AI. They allow us to see the potential dangers of AI, even if they are exaggerated.

Terminator 2 was the most impactful AI movie of my childhood. In the film, the artificial intelligence of the future becomes powerful enough to take over the world. Humanity's only hope lies in a cyborg assassin sent from the future to protect them.

I remember watching Terminator 1 and 2 as a kid. Why my parents let me watch an "R" rated horror movie at ten years old is a discussion for another day.

Unfortunately, this 30-year-old storyline, and others like it that have followed, has shaped the public perception of AI. This movie effectively ingrained in many viewers a deep-seated fear of robots taking over the world and mercilessly slaughtering humans.

While we may have real AI technologies today that continue to get better and better, this sci-fi story remains a fantasy.

But fantasies can still serve as warnings. It is up to good people to responsibly harness this technology.

Despite popular misconceptions and fears, countless examples exist of people and businesses using AI ethically and effectively.

That's the stuff I will be helping you with. I want you to be one of the good ones in the story. This opportunity can reshape the public's opinion of AI and show that it can make positive societal changes that help us all live better lives.

WHAT YOU CAN EXPECT TO LEARN

Part One brings you up to speed with what AI is already doing for small businesses and society at large, provides helpful definitions for standard AI terms and technologies, and highlights some of the most-used technologies in the business world.

Part Two helps you set the foundation for beginning the AI integration process for your small business, provides examples of AI tools and platforms, and guides you through managing change and discussing AI with your team.

Part Three outlines the importance of ethical considerations when using AI, establishes the Ten Commandments of ethical AI use, and discusses the risks you face when using AI in your small business.

BECAUSE I LOVE SMALL BUSINESSES LIKE YOURS

It's well-documented that too many small businesses face closure within their first few years. Business consultants love to quote these statistics. Here they are one more time:

About 20% of small businesses fail within the first year.

- 30% of small businesses fail within the second year. Around 50% of small businesses fail by the end of the fifth year.
- 70% of small businesses fail by the end of the tenth year.

The reasons for small business despair are myriad: cash flow challenges, evolving market needs, stiff competition, or, sometimes, unforeseen events that shift economic sands overnight (remember that horrible pandemic we all had to go through?).

As a business owner, I know these aren't just numbers or faceless statistics. They represent dreams, grit, and tireless nights of hard work. They're emblematic of your sacrifices, the family events you might miss, and the personal savings you've likely invested.

I've had the privilege to sit across tables from many of you, hearing your stories, ambitions, and fears about your business (and AI). Every story is unique, yet there's a common thread — a relentless spirit and a dream to help more people and build a better life for your family.

You've worked so hard and you're concerned some AI technology could wipe it overnight. I get that.

The weight you bear as a small business owner is enormous, balancing the livelihoods of your employees with the survival and growth of your dream. The resilience you display in the face of adversity these past years and the passion you bring to your community is not just commendable, it's inspirational.

My heart goes out to you in your dedication and hard work. I sincerely hope the insights and wisdom shared in these pages can serve as a beacon in your journey.

I believe AI is going to help people like us.

Small businesses are society's heartbeat, providing jobs, solving problems, and feeding families. They also play an integral role in keeping the economy going. I take great pride in helping entrepreneurs succeed.

I'm a champion of AI because I am a champion of the small business owner. I think it's going to help us succeed and get to spend more time doing the things we want to. The right tools will give small business owners more time at home and more money in their pockets.

I'm passionate about helping businesses use AI technology to their advantage. My goal is to provide you with an understanding of AI and practical strategies to get the most out of existing resources.

You'll soon learn what AI is. You'll get ideas about how to save time, improve decision-making, and unlock new creative opportunities for growth and success.

That's how AI works. But let's start by developing an understanding of what AI is.

---

1. Dell'Acqua, F., & Rajendran, S. (2023). Navigating the jagged technological frontier: Field experimental evidence of the effects of AI on knowledge worker productivity and quality. Harvard Business School & Boston Consulting Group.
2. Ibid

3. Data derived from historical technology adoption rates and recent platform user statistics. Exact sources might vary based on the data's origin and its update after 2021. https://chat.openai.com/c/7f260878-b597-4793-a5d7-1fff25f1bd09#user-content-fnref-1%5E

4. McKinsey Global Institute. (2018). Notes from the AI frontier: Modeling the impact of AI on the world economy. https://www.mckinsey.com/featured-insights/artificial-intelligence/notes-from-the-ai-frontier-modeling-the-impact-of-ai-on-the-world-economy

5. Brynjolfsson, E., & Li, D. (2023). Generative AI at Work. NBER. https://www.nber.org/papers/w31161

   See also: Nielsen, J. (2023, July 16). AI Improves Employee Productivity by 66%. NNGroup. https://www.nngroup.com/articles/ai-tools-productivity-gains/

6. SMB Group. (2021). 2021 Small and Medium Business Digital Transformation Study. https://www.smb-gr.com/.s

7. McKinsey & Company. (2023). Generative AI and the future of work in America. Retrieved from https://www.mckinsey.com/mgi/our-research/generative-ai-and-the-future-of-work-in-america#/

PART ONE
AI BASICS

1 WHAT AI CAN DO AND WILL DO

Most small business owners begin their venture with a simple dream: *to improve our world by creating something of value for others.*

Starting a business is risky, and every entrepreneur needs to use all available tools if they are going to fulfill their dreams and do their part to build a better world for their customers.

Initially, we rely on sweat equity to build a business. We roll up our sleeves, put in the hours, and get the job done. But as time passes, we find better ways to work. We remove inefficiencies. We solve problems faster. We get more focused on what works. We even begin to embrace new tools and technologies that make work easier and more efficient.

The best businesses have always capitalized on new tools: steam power, electricity, airplanes, and, of course, the Internet!

These innovations have allowed us to move faster, help more people, and scale our businesses.

Each generation has eventually embraced this new technology with excitement, tempered by caution—knowing full well its potential for causing disruption and progress in society.

Small business owners have always been at the forefront of embracing new technology to improve their lives and businesses. From the Industrial Revolution to the digital age, they have sought out new technologies that could help them save time, increase productivity, and ultimately make life more convenient for themselves and others.

This willingness to embrace change has resulted in innovative products and services that have transformed entire industries.

The rise of artificial intelligence is no exception. It's a new tool in our belts as small business owners. By embracing this new technology, we can stay ahead of the curve, provide value to our customers, and save ourselves time to increase business success further.

You might feel like AI has suddenly been thrown in your face. The truth is, it's been around for a long time. You may not have realized it, but AI is being used around you, making your life a little easier.

A BRIEF HISTORY LESSON IN AI

The term "Artificial Intelligence" was first coined by John McCarthy for the 1956 Dartmouth Conference, an event credited as the birthplace of AI as an academic discipline.[1] At this gathering, leading thinkers like Alan Turing, Marvin Minsky, Allen Newell, and Herbert Simon began pioneering research, laying the groundwork for AI. Turing's 1950 paper "Computing Machinery and Intelligence" had previously introduced the idea of machines that could mimic human intelligence, proposing what is now known as the Turing Test.[2]

Over the decades, AI witnessed several seasons of optimism followed by "AI winters" marked by skepticism and reduced funding. The field oscillated between periods of advancement and stagnation.

Recently, AI has undergone a remarkable renaissance. It's everywhere, whether we realize it or not. Let's look at some everyday examples you'll be familiar with.

INDUSTRY LEADERS ADOPTING AI TECHNOLOGY

Leading businesses use AI to develop new ideas, make communication smoother, and make their customers happier. However you feel about AI today, it's already all around you. Like a fish in water, modern society swims in the waters of AI.

Let's briefly look at how four big companies are using AI to improve their businesses and make our lives a little easier.

- *Amazon*: Amazon uses AI to automate processes, including customer recommendation engines and warehouse systems for product management.
- *Apple*: Apple leverages its proprietary Siri technology to provide users with personalized recommendations based on their preferences and interests. Additionally, they use AI to power their facial recognition software and automated responses when you call customer service.
- *Google*: Google utilizes AI in several areas of its business, including image searches, natural language processing, and self-driving cars. They also use machine learning algorithms to quickly improve search accuracy and identify spam emails.
- *Uber*: Uber uses advanced AI technologies such as machine vision to automatically detect unusual rider behavior or suspicious activities and alert drivers accordingly—significantly improving safety for both riders and drivers.

The narrative that AI is only for the "big players" is a limiting one. It's akin to those who predicted that, computers were just for large corporations or that the Internet would only benefit multinational companies. We all know how those stories turned out. Just as computers have become an everyday presence and the Internet is now essential for all, AI is rapidly evolving into a tool that businesses of all sizes can and should embrace.

YOUR SMALL BUSINESS ADVANTAGE

In many aspects, small businesses are well-positioned to benefit from AI in ways that even large enterprises might envy. With their agility, flexibility, and often a closer relationship with their customer base, small businesses can utilize AI tools to quickly adapt to market changes, understand customer behavior, and even predict future trends.

Soon, AI will no longer seem like a buzzword or an unreachable tool preserved for tech giants. Instead, it will emerge as your secret weapon — a force multiplier in your quest to stand out, and thrive in the small business world. AI for you will be a powerful, game-changing tool that can significantly amplify the effectiveness and success of your small businesses in a competitive and rapidly evolving market. This future is neither distant nor reserved for the few; it's here and accessible right now.

While we don't have these giant enterprises' development budgets, we can still see that AI is already part of how we serve our customers. To ignore it is to fall behind and lose touch with how business is and will be done. To embrace it is to align our business practice with the current of where technology and culture have gone. An openness to accept technology is a big part of this. We will get left behind if we don't keep changing and growing. The business world moves fast, and we've got to roll with it.

Instead of it being a tool of big tech, I believe AI is the great leveler of the playing field.

When competitive edges are razor-thin, AI's "skill leveling" effect can be the difference-maker for small businesses. By democratizing expertise and breaking down traditional barriers, AI promises to usher in an era where the size of a business doesn't dictate its potential. With AI in their corner, small businesses can dream big, achieve bigger, and redefine what's possible in the business realm.

The concept of "skill leveling" is a testament to AI's power to democratize expertise. Hiring top-tier talent can be a significant challenge for small businesses due to budget constraints or the intense competition for such expertise in the market. But a new study found that AI can help less experienced workers improve their performance by 43%. This discovery opens up exciting possibilities for the future.[3]

WOULD YOU GET HELP FROM DR. CHAT?

I smile when I hear my American friends and clients raving about how wonderful healthcare is in Canada. It may be ok, but it is far from perfect. In fact, as a parent of young kids in Canada, it's terrible sometimes. Finding a doctor in Canada is so tough. The wait times are ludicrous, and the whole system is strained to the point that many experts are calling for an overhaul.

To state the obvious: *The Canadian healthcare system needs some serious help.*

AI could be that help.

AI is going to help a ton of parents get some of the help they need as quickly as possible. A recent study compared how a physician and an AI chatbot answered patient questions. The study randomly drew 195 exchanges from October 2022, where a verified physician responded to a public inquiry. Chatbot responses were generated by entering the original question into a fresh session in December 2022. A team of licensed healthcare professionals then evaluated the responses provided by both the physician and the chatbot. The results were genuinely eye-opening to how much AI can help this struggling sector of society:

- Evaluators preferred chatbot responses to physician responses in 78.6% of the 585 evaluations.
- Physician responses were significantly shorter than chatbot responses (52 words vs. 211 words on average).
- Chatbot responses were rated of significantly higher quality than physician responses. Specifically, 78.5% of chatbot responses were rated as good or very good quality, compared to 22.1% for physicians.

- Chatbot responses were also rated significantly more empathetic than physician responses. The proportion of responses rated empathetic or very empathetic was higher for chatbots (45.1%) than for physicians (4.6%).[4]

I'm certainly not saying that we don't need human doctors anymore. This advancement suggests that AI chatbots can significantly improve the healthcare system by providing reliable information to patients. This could help ease the workload of healthcare professionals and ultimately lead to better outcomes for patients.

This advancement in AI, as demonstrated by the study, also points to a broader potential: freeing up healthcare professionals to focus on higher-value activities. For instance, by handling routine inquiries, AI chatbots can significantly reduce the time doctors spend on administrative tasks, allowing them to dedicate more attention to complex patient care.

A recent development in Quebec further illustrates this shift towards efficiency. The region eliminated a specific form in the healthcare system, reportedly unlocking the potential for 10,000 additional patient visits. This example underscores how reducing paperwork and administrative burdens can have a substantial impact on patient care. By integrating AI into our healthcare system, we can further amplify these benefits, ensuring that healthcare professionals have more time for direct patient care and other critical activities that require their expertise and human touch.[5]

JOINING FORCES WITH AI

The advent of artificial intelligence has been revolutionary—yet the most meaningful human interactions still rely on us. Our connections, relationships, creativity, empathy, and problem-solving skills drive progress in the world far more than technological advancements.

This doesn't mean AI isn't necessary—far from it.

After all, artificial intelligence is becoming increasingly sophisticated, taking on complex tasks and aiding us in our daily lives. But when it comes to interpersonal relationships, deep thought processes, and creative breakthroughs, human beings will provide the touch of excellence that can elevate anything from average results to extraordinary successes.

The future lies in combining the best of both worlds: human intelligence *plus* artificial intelligence.

Human ingenuity combined with AI technology can achieve remarkable heights, elevating tasks with a powerful combination of intelligence and experience. When these two forces come together as one entity, we witness true magic occur.

DON'T GET LEFT BEHIND

From the invention of the wheel to the rise of the Internet, technological innovation has been the driving force behind human progress. Those who fail to evolve will eventually become irrelevant and fade into obscurity.

I'm not talking about how you interact with friends and family. I'm talking about how you engage in the marketplace. AI is helping those who are willing to receive its help. AI has the potential to automate mundane tasks faster than humans, allowing anyone to not only cut costs but also improve the speed of their operations.

This does not mean human skills are no longer necessary. Human workers will still be vital in many ways.

While some may fear that AI will take their job, the reality is that it is much more likely to transform their roles. We still need people to think outside the box and develop innovative solutions—something machines can't do. By leveraging machine and human capabilities, businesses will gain a competitive advantage while staying cost-effective and efficient.

Simply put, businesses not embracing AI technology risk being left behind. Companies that fail to invest in AI and learn to integrate it into their daily operations effectively will find it significantly harder to compete with those who have.

As AI takes care of routine tasks that take up our time, the demand for skills that AI cannot replicate — such as creative thinking, complex problem-solving, relationships, and emotional intelligence — is likely to rise. Those who fail to complement AI technologies with these uniquely human skills risk losing their competitive edge in the work-force. Simply put, they will be spending too much time doing what others have outsourced to AI that they won't have time to do the tasks that really "move the needle" in life and business.

It gets more pressing. The reluctance or inability to adapt to AI-driven changes will lead to a widening skills gap. This gap not only affects individual career prospects but could also lead to broader social and economic disparities. As some segments of the workforce advance with AI, others may struggle to keep pace, potentially leading to increased unemployment or underemployment in certain sectors.

Therefore, it's crucial for individuals, just as for businesses, to embrace what AI is offering. This means investing in continuous learning and skill development, staying abreast of technological advancements, and cultivating an adaptive mindset. By doing so, they can ensure that they remain valuable and relevant in an AI-integrated future, where human ingenuity and AI's efficiency combine to create new opportunities and drive innovation forward.

A TIME FOR REINVENTION

Let's imagine two hypothetical companies in a hypothetical situation: Johnson & Associates and Smith & Co. These two companies competed to be the industry leader. While both firms were successful, they had different approaches to technology, particularly their use of AI.

Johnson & Associates was an old-school firm that prioritized human expertise over technology. They believed hard work and human-driven research were always superior (and safer) than AI tools. Some of their concerns were legitimate, but they should have taken more risks. Contrary to what the younger partners suggested, the senior partners saw it as a threat to their traditional methods.

Meanwhile, Smith & Co saw the potential of AI and invested in AI-powered legal software. The results were outstanding. The system streamlined their paperwork and allowed them to handle more cases simultaneously. It's not that the technology replaced their human team members; instead, it allowed them to take on more cases, help more people, and do so in less time. As a result, their lawyers could spend more time with clients instead of working on tedious administrative tasks.

As time went by, Smith & Co surpassed Johnson & Associates in every measure of success. The firm's investment in AI gave them a competitive edge, enabling them to say "Yes" to more projects and reduce paper usage while providing faster, more cost-effective services. Their personalized approach appealed to younger clients who appreciated the firm's responsiveness and communication.

Eventually, Johnson & Associates became slower, more expensive, and unable to adapt to the constantly evolving needs of their clients.

The lesson from this story is clear: *Businesses must stay at the forefront of technological changes or risk falling behind their competitors.* By integrating AI technologies, firms can offer their customers improved accuracy, faster service, lower costs, and better communication. In today's competitive world, embracing AI is essential for companies that want to thrive and expand their customer base.

Adapt or fall behind. By leveraging the power of AI, small businesses can provide better service, make informed decisions, and stay ahead of the competition. The question is, will you be like Johnson & Associates and resist change, or will you embrace AI like Smith & Co and dominate the competition?

The choice is yours.

1. Smith, C., McGuire, B., Huang, T., & Yang, G. (2006, December). *The History of Artificial Intelligence.* In CSEP 590A: History of Computing. University of Washington.
2. The Turing Test, proposed by the British mathematician and computer scientist Alan Turing in 1950, is a benchmark to determine a machine's ability to exhibit intelligent behavior indistinguishable from that of a human. In the test, a human evaluator engages in a natural language conversation with both a human and a machine designed to generate human-like responses. If the evaluator cannot reliably distinguish which participant is the machine, then the machine is considered to have passed the test and demonstrated a form of artificial intelligence. From Russell, S. J., & Norvig, P. (2020). Artificial intelligence: A modern approach. Malaysia; Pearson Education Limited.
3. Brynjolfsson, E., & Li, D. (2023). Generative AI at Work. NBER. https://www.nber.org/papers/w31161
4. Ayers, J. W. (2023). Comparing Physician and Artificial Intelligence Chatbot Responses to Patient Questions Posted to a Public Social Media Forum. JAMA Internal Medicine, 183(6), 589-596. https://doi.org/10.1001/jamainternmed.2023.1838
5. "Quebec unveils major plan to reform health-care system ahead of election". Reported by CTV News. March 30, 2022. https://montreal.ctvnews.ca/quebec-unveils-major-plan-to-reform-health-care-system-ahead-of-election-1.5838903

2 WHAT IS AI REALLY?

Have you ever been fascinated by how things work? Think back to your childhood – was there a moment when your curiosity led you to dismantle a toy or a gadget, just to peek at its inner workings? This universal curiosity, the desire to understand and explore, is something that connects all of us.

Curiosity is a foundational trait to understanding AI. You have to come at it with an open mind. That's one of the many things my mentor, Ted Lasso taught me.

TED LASSO DELIVERS A REAL GEM

I was so sad when the show, Ted Lasso ended. I loved it all, even the episodes that weren't as good - I still loved them. I loved the main character, Ted Lasso, one of the best characters in TV history. Let's draw inspiration from a scene from the hit Apple TV+, Emmy award winning series. For those who haven't seen the show, it's a heart-warming and humorous series about an American football coach, Ted Lasso, who moves to the U.K. to coach a British football team. Despite his lack of soccer experience, Ted's unflagging optimism and unconventional methods make a significant impact on all he meets.

In one memorable scene, Ted engages in a game of darts with Rupert, the former team owner and villain of the series. Throughout their inter-action, Ted recalls a moment that shaped his perspective on life. He shares a quote he once saw, 'Be curious, not judgmental,' credited to Walt Whitman. This quote strikes at the core of Ted's approach – he emphasizes that those who underestimated him lacked curiosity, choosing to judge rather than inquire and understand.

This scene, though from a show about football, holds relevance to our exploration of AI. Just as Ted was underestimated in his dart-playing abilities due to a lack of curiosity, the field of AI is often approached with preconceived notions and judgments. To truly grasp AI's poten-tial, we must be curious.

In the context of AI, this translates to the need for us to explore beyond surface-level knowledge and common myths.

BE PROUD OF CURIOSITY

Curiosity led me to AI. As a kid, I never resisted the urge to explore the inner workings of everyday items.

Throughout my childhood, my fascination with electronic gadgets led me to conduct a series of makeshift experiments. I remember one day when I took apart my parents' old radio to figure out why it had stopped working. I had no idea how radios worked, but my curiosity knew no bounds. I took the radio apart and examined each piece. Though I had no idea what I was doing, it was interesting to see how everything worked together.

Fast forward to today, and my childhood curiosity has evolved into an interest (and sometimes distraction) in cutting-edge technologies like AI. Just like back then, I've realized that understanding the fundamen-tals of the parts is crucial to getting your head around its whole. Though I'll never be a software engineer or developer, knowing how AI works and the key terms associated with it is our first step to making informed decisions.

WHAT IS AI?

AI, at its core, is about machines simulating human intelligence, making decisions, and learning from data. When we talk about AI, we use terms like machine learning, neural networks, and natural language processing. While these words may seem daunting, knowing these concepts is an essential step in enabling us to effectively leverage AI tools and navigate the ever-changing business landscape.

In the same way I took apart that old radio to learn how it worked, understanding the mechanisms and definitions of AI empowers us to make the best use of its potential, make informed choices, and confidently discuss AI applications in the business world.

During my research of what AI is, I realized there was this whole dictionary of new terms that I had to figure out. The talking heads and gurus all said them so quickly as if everyone knew them. But I didn't know them. And even after studying their definitions, I still didn't know them.

If you're like me, you need complex things explained simply with as many analogies and word pictures as possible. I'm going to share with you how I've made sense of the many terms you hear in AI circles.

I'll do my best to break down the AI jargon for you. Why? Because informed decisions are smart decisions. With clarity, you'll not only protect yourself from opportunistic vendors looking to make a quick buck from you, but you'll also be able to engage in meaningful conversations about how AI can truly benefit your business.

I want to make sure you have all the knowledge you need to not just survive but thrive in this era of shiny new tools.

AN AI DEFINITION I LIKE

Ask ten different AI experts what the definition of AI is, and you'll get twelve different answers. That's not very helpful for our discussion.

A consulting group working for the U.S. government published an insightful report about AI that provided a helpful definition. They described AI as:

> A machine-based system capable of influencing its environment by producing outputs like predictions, recommendations, or decisions. It uses data to perceive environments, abstract perceptions into models, and uses model inference to formulate outcomes.[1]

That definition might be a bit too wordy for now. So, imagine a computer that can watch, listen, and learn from things just like we do. It takes in information, like how you might learn facts for a school quiz, and then uses that to make smart choices or predictions. Let's say you always play a certain game every Saturday. An AI might notice that pattern and if you asked it what day you will play it again, it would answer "Saturday." It's using what it knows to answer a question. That's a simple explanation of AI. But complex ideas call us to go deeper, and so we must heed it.

THE TWO KINDS OF AI YOU NEED TO KNOW

Despite its broad definition, AI is classified into two categories: artificial narrow intelligence (ANI) and artificial general intelligence (AGI). One is already a mainstay in society. The other could spell the end of human history and is the fodder for science fiction movies that haunt us. Let's talk about each of these terms so you can see what all the fuss is about.

1. Artificial Narrow Intelligence

Artificial narrow intelligence (we just say "ANI" for short) is a specialized form of AI that excels in performing a singular task. Its capabilities are confined to the specific domain it's designed for, and it doesn't possess the ability to think, reason, or make decisions outside of that domain. It sounds crass but it's a dumb technology. It just obeys what its code tells it to do.

Imagine a highly skilled artisan who has mastered crafting one particular item to perfection but doesn't have knowledge or expertise in any other craft. They're a genius at art but useless at sports, math, or any kind of relationship. We all know people like that. That's ANI for you – an expert in one domain but limited to just that.

How Does ANI Work?

In my own journey of understanding AI, I became a champion of ANI. If I was to do this in public, I wanted to know everything about it. Here are some characteristics of ANI I think you should know about:

It follows the rules and systems: ANI is rooted and governed by its programming. People put rules into the code of ANI so it knows what to do. As a parent, sometimes I wish I could code certain behaviours into my children so that they always behaved exactly like I wanted them too. Anyone with kids knows that this is not a thing. Children have agency. This means regardless of what you tell them, they will still do what they want (and give their parents grey hair in the process). ANI is not like my children - it always does what it is told. At the heart of ANI lies a set of predefined rules and algorithms. These rules dictate the AI's behavior and responses. For example, a spell-checker in word processing software is a form of ANI. It follows linguistic rules set by the most annoying grammar police you've ever met. It has been trained to identify and correct spelling mistakes.

It learns from data: Some ANI systems can learn from data to improve performance. For instance, a spam filter in your email learns from the emails you mark as spam and then avoids sending them again. Over time, it gets better at identifying and blocking unwanted emails from foreign princes who insist you claim your long-lasting inheritance.

It doesn't transfer knowledge: One of the defining characteristics of ANI is its inability to transfer knowledge from one domain to another. If you have a data set about how to drive a car safely, that data will be restricted to driving. It cannot take insights learned from driving and apply it to, for example, playing chess. A chess-playing ANI can't use its knowledge of chess to drive a car or play poker. Each task requires a separate ANI system, specifically designed and trained for its use.

Task-specific algorithms: ANI is often powered by algorithms tailored for its specific task. It uses a set of step-by-step instructions called an "algorithm" to do the job. Think of this like a recipe. Just as a recipe tells you exactly what to do to make cookies, an algorithm tells ANI precisely how to do its job.

ANI is a testament to the power of specialization. While it doesn't possess the broad cognitive abilities that many envision when considering AI, its precision and efficiency in its designated domain often surpass human capabilities. For businesses and individuals alike, understanding and harnessing the potential of ANI can lead to significant advancements and improvements in specific tasks and operations.

Some well-recognized use cases of ANI are:

Chatbots: Many businesses use chatbots on their websites to answer frequently asked questions. These chatbots are programmed with a set of responses to specific queries.

Recommendation systems: How do streaming services like Netflix or Spotify suggest shows, movies, or songs? They use ANI to analyze your preferences and suggest content accordingly. Google uses narrow AI in its search algorithms and in the "People also searched for..." sections. Netflix uses AI to help you decide what to watch—with the "Because you watched..." feature.

Email filtering: Your email service's ability to sort emails into "Primary," "Social," and "Promotions" tabs is another example of ANI at work. Email platforms on Google, Microsoft, and Apple have implemented AI-driven spelling recommendations so people don't have to know how bad your spelling is.

Voice assistants: Voice assistants like Amazon's Alexa or Apple's Siri are advanced forms of ANI. They use AI in their natural language processing capabilities to perform a range of tasks but within a defined scope. Your phone also uses ANI to recognize your face and carry out tasks for you.

2. Artificial General Intelligence

Artificial general intelligence (AGI) is the kind of AI you've likely seen in movies. It's a hypothetical intelligent system designed to mimic the abilities of the human brain. The primary objective of AGI is to understand and emulate human intelligence, including language comprehension, problem-solving skills, creative thinking, and learning from experience.

AGI is considered to be the next frontier in AI, but many experts believe that it will be many years before we achieve it, if at all.[2]

With AGI, a system could perform tasks that have not been programmed in advance. This ability sets AGI apart from other AI technologies based on narrow AI, like machine learning or deep learning. Machines equipped with AGI technology can analyze vast amounts of data in real-time, make informed decisions, and predict and adapt to environmental changes. It would also interact with humans in a more meaningful and intuitive manner.

Why Don't We Have AGI Yet?

While AGI technology holds tremendous potential, its development is a complex and multi-faceted problem. Currently, humanity has yet to create a fully functional AGI system. Many in the development community are working tirelessly to improve AI technologies and push the boundaries of what is possible with AGI. However, most experts believe that it may take many more years to achieve a complete AGI system, *if it's possible at all.*[3]

There are several reasons for this delay. First, the human brain is one of the most complex structures in the universe. Scientists have spent years on it and are still trying to understand how it works. Secondly, we do not yet have the computing power or algorithms to support AGI. Third and finally, the international community needs to figure out ethical and safety concerns associated with AGI. Machines that can make their own decisions have the potential to be extremely dangerous if not properly designed or managed.

Despite the potential challenges, AGI still represents the goal of many. We still have a long way to go before we are close to achieving it. The development of AGI requires significant advancements in computer science, neuroscience, and philosophy. It also requires us to carefully consider the ethical and safety implications of creating machines that can make their own decisions.

At this point, AGI will be left to the realm of researchers, ethicists, and the deepest fears of those who see you reading a book about why we should embrace AI. Since this is a business book, we won't be talking about AGI anymore. We're going to stay very practical.

BEING CURIOUS *AND* INSPIRED

As we reach the end of this chapter, it's clear that the world of Artificial Narrow Intelligence (ANI) is not just a futuristic concept, but a present reality enhancing many aspects of our lives. I encourage you to take a moment and look around. Observe the subtle yet significant ways ANI is already making your life easier and more efficient.

Is it the voice assistant on your phone that sets your alarms and reminders? Or the smart thermostat in your home that learns your preferences and adjusts the temperature accordingly? Perhaps it's the way your social media feeds seem to know exactly the kind of content you like, or how your email filters out spam before it reaches your inbox. These are all examples of ANI at work – specialized, efficient, and often operating so seamlessly that we take their presence for granted.

Let this realization be a call to action. Reflect on how these ANI applications impact your daily routine and think about how their underlying principles can be applied in other areas of your life or business. This exercise is not just about appreciating technology; it's about embracing a mindset of curiosity and innovation – traits that are essential as we navigate the constantly evolving landscape of AI.

And in the spirit of Ted Lasso, remember: 'Be curious, not judgmental.' Approach the world of AI with an open, inquisitive mind. Let's not just passively observe the wonders of ANI, but actively engage with it, understanding their workings and dreaming up new possibilities in your business.

Who knows, by embracing this Ted Lasso/ Walt Whitman curiosity, you might discover new ways ANI can further enhance your life or business – and that's a goal worth scoring.

As we conclude this chapter, let's carry forward this curiosity, looking at AI not just as a tool or a concept, but as a companion in our journey towards innovation and improvement. The world of ANI is here, making our lives better in countless ways – let's recognize it, appreciate it, and be inspired by it.

---

1. U.S.-EU Trade and Technology Council. (2022). The Impact of Artificial Intelligence on the Future of Workforces in the European Union and the United States of America. White House. https://www.whitehouse.gov/wp-content/uploads/2022/12/TTC-EC-CEA-AI-Report-12052022-1.pdf

2. Suleyman, M. (2023). It's imperative – and nearly impossible – to contain artificial intelligence, expert says. Marketplace. Retrieved from https://www.marketplace.org/shows/marketplace-tech/its-imperative-and-nearly-impossible-to-contain-artificial-intelligence-expert-says/?n=@

3. There are two recommended resources to explore on this important topic.

   Levin, John-Clark & Maas, Matthijs M. (2020). "Roadmap to a Roadmap: How Could We Tell When AGI is a 'Manhattan Project' Away?". This paper discusses the potential for a clear roadmap to emerge for achieving AGI, suggesting that a focused effort similar to the Manhattan Project could expedite its realization. The authors also explore the implications of such a threshold for AI risks and international governance.

   Allyn-Feuer, Ari & Sanders, Ted (2023). "Transformative AGI by 2043 is <1% likely". In this paper, the authors estimate the likelihood of achieving transformative AGI by 2043 to be less than 1%. They argue that the bar for AGI is high and requires many steps, each with its own set of challenges and probabilities.

3 AI-RELATED TERMS YOU NEED TO KNOW

I f you're like me, you don't like to look or sound like an idiot. To combat this, I work hard to keep up with the times. I watch the news. I keep up with social media. I also pay attention to how I dress, groom, and behave in public. I want to look competent around respectable people.

This is never more at risk than when I'm discussing wine among polite company and dining at a restaurant. I'm out of my area of expertise in this scenario. Experience has now armed me with a few pretentious terms I've picked up. With words like 'tannins', 'full bodied', and 'oaky', I can now nod with the best of them and avoid looking completely out of my depth.

As an aside, I'm still not satisfied on the word 'dry' for wines. We already have an understanding of what 'dry' means. If I spill a 'dry' wine it on my shirt, it definitely won't be dry. We are using the wrong word. Wine is the opposite of dry. It's a liquid. But there I am, swirling my glass like I know what I'm doing, agreeing wholeheartedly, 'Ah yes, quite dry, just how I like it.'

Of course, I'll never say this to a wine expert. They've already thrown the book across the room and sent me an email insisting, "Dry is the taste in your mouth after you drink it!"

Fine. Something happens in your mouth when you drink that kind of wine. But it's not dry. Your mouth is a cesspool of all kinds of moisture. It's not dry. We need another word.

As you can imagine, I don't have ambitions to be a sommelier. But knowing just a bit more than the red-white dichotomy definitely helps in not looking like I missed the 'Wine 101' class in Adulting School.

I include this confession because it's also how we can feel about AI. Unlike knowing a lot about wine, understanding AI words does have some actual value. You don't need to know everything, but understanding a bit - like the difference between machine learning and a sentient robot apocalypse – can make you sound intelligent in a conversation. It could open doors of opportunity for you. That's what I seek to help you with here.

WHY AI IS LIKE A FINE WINE

The connection between AI and wine is not about time. It's about knowing enough to stay relevant. If you're like me and want to sound like you know what you're talking about, you must learn a few things about AI. And since everyone is talking about AI these days, I want us to be able to know what they're talking about. Maybe, after all this, we will have something insightful to contribute.

When you read or hear people talking about AI, you may come across some confusing terms. Instead of being intimidated or overwhelmed, consider it a learning opportunity. Understanding key terms will enhance your understanding of AI and how your small businesses can leverage it.

I'll be using these words in the coming chapters as well. It will be tough to get your head around AI and how you can integrate it without knowing some of the common terms used.

You can use this next section as a glossary that you can reference whenever you want. It's good to feel like you understand some of the terms used so that you feel intelligent when considering integrating it or when you find yourself in a conversation about AI.

Machine Learning (ML)

Machine learning is a subset of AI that enables systems to learn from data and improve their performance without being explicitly programmed, often through algorithms.

Machine learning is a type of AI that involves training computers to learn from data and make decisions without being programmed. It involves feeding large amounts of data into algorithms and models to enable computers to learn to identify patterns and make predictions.

Data

Imagine data as the vast library of books that AI systems read. Just as we gain knowledge from reading books, AI learns from consuming data. Every piece of data is like a page in a book, providing information and insights. The more books (or data) AI reads, the more knowledgeable and informed it becomes. Data can come from various sources: pictures, texts, numbers, and even our online behaviors. It's the raw material that AI uses to understand patterns, make predictions, and offer solutions. Just as a chef needs the right ingredients to make a delicious meal, AI needs quality data to produce accurate and helpful results. Without data, AI is like a library without books; it can't function or provide answers.

Big Data

Big data is like normal data, just bigger.

Imagine that massive library full of books, but now we will add to it. Instead of just books, this library has videos, photos, and recordings, all stacked up in enormous quantities. This vast collection is what we call big data. It's not just about the size but the variety and speed at which new information gets added. Traditional methods like trying to read every book individually won't work here. We need special tools, like super-fast reading machines, to go through everything and find the information we need. Just as a huge library would need advanced systems to catalog and locate specific books, big data requires specialized technologies to store, process, and make sense of all the information it holds.

Parameters

A parameter, in the context of AI and machine learning, is like a tiny piece of knowledge or a computer's setting to make decisions. Imagine if your brain had tiny knobs for learning different things, and by adjusting each knob, you can remember or understand better. In AI, each knob is a parameter, and the computer adjusts these knobs to get better at its job. The more knobs (or parameters) it has, the more it can learn and remember.

Think of a parameter as a tiny dial or setting inside a computer program. When the program starts, it might not have the dials set just right. As the computer uses the program, it sees how well it's doing and adjusts these dials to do even better. It gets its feedback from the data it processes. So, as the computer sees more data and learns from it, it tweaks the dials, or parameters, to become more accurate in its predictions or decisions. It's like fine-tuning a musical instrument to get the perfect sound.

Deep Learning

Think of the human brain as a vast city with numerous interconnected roads and pathways. Each road represents a connection or a "neuron," and the entire city represents our brain's network. This intricate city-like structure of our brain inspires deep learning. It uses something called "artificial neural networks" to mimic these pathways. Just as different routes in a city help us reach various destinations, these artificial networks help the computer process and understand complex data, like pictures and voices. For instance, when you show a computer many pictures of cats, it uses these networks to recognize patterns and features, like whiskers or tails. Over time, just as we learn the best routes in a city, the computer learns to identify a cat in any new picture. Deep learning is exceptionally adept at tasks like image recognition or understanding spoken words, making it a powerful tool in AI.

Automation

Imagine a factory where toys are made. In the past, every toy was crafted by hand, requiring a lot of time and effort from workers. But then, machines were introduced. These machines could produce toys faster without getting tired. Now, think of automation as an even more advanced factory, where not only are toys made, but the machines can also decide which toys to produce based on what's popular, fix themselves if they break, and even order materials when they run out. All of this happens without much human intervention. Just as machines in the factory make the toy-making process smoother and more efficient, automation, with the help of AI and ML, takes care of repetitive tasks and decisions in various fields. This means tasks are done faster and more accurately, and humans can focus on more complex and creative aspects.

Generative AI

Generative AI gets its information from large amounts of data that it is trained on. For instance, if you want the AI to generate new images of cats, you would first show it thousands or even millions of cat images. The AI studies these images, learns patterns, features, and styles from them, and then uses what it has learned to create new cat images. The same goes for other types of data, like text or music. The more data you provide to the AI, the better it becomes at generating new, similar content. The data it learns from is often called a "training dataset."

The best example of generative AI is in OpenAI's Chat-GPT evolution. Initial models were trained on limited text datasets, which meant they had constraints in understanding context and producing coherent responses. The leap came with GPT (Generative Pre-trained Transformer), which marked a significant advancement. The term "pretrained" signifies that it underwent training on a vast amount of text data from the Internet before being fine-tuned for specific tasks. This foundational training allowed it to learn grammar, facts, reasoning abilities, and even some biases from the data.

As the models evolved, each version was fed more data and became increasingly sophisticated. GPT-2, for instance, could generate much more coherent and diverse paragraphs of text. GPT-3, with its 175 billion parameters, showcased a breadth of capabilities from drafting essays to creating poetry and even writing rudimentary software code. This progression underlines a central tenet: by training on expansive and diverse text data from the Internet, the model becomes more knowledgeable and can emulate human-like text based on its training. The continual growth in data and algorithm refinements makes each iteration more versatile and capable.

Predictive Analytics

Each year, farmers predict the best time to plant their crops. With enough experience and information, they can make better decisions. They look back at old journals, noting when the crops produced best in previous years. Then, they consider weather patterns and other phenomena that could affect the harvest. Over time, they see patterns and can make educated guesses about the best planting times for the upcoming seasons. Predictive analytics is like this farmer but on a much grander scale. Instead of journals, it uses vast amounts of historical data. Instead of relying on human intuition, it uses learning algorithms. By analyzing past events and trends, predictive analytics can forecast future outcomes, whether predicting business sales, finding a disease that is undetectable by human analysis, or even the next big trend in fashion. This foresight helps companies and individuals make informed decisions, ensuring they're always a step ahead.

Algorithm

An algorithm is a set of rules and instructions for an AI to follow. Similarly to how we use a flow chart, an algorithm tells the computer what decisions it can make with the given data.

Google uses the most famous algorithm. Most people, understandably, have no idea why Google ranks one site over another. How does it know the best results to give you when you ask a question of it? Think of Google as a super-smart librarian in the most extensive library in the world. This library has billions of books. Every day, new books are added. People come to this librarian for the best book on a specific topic.

First, before anyone even asks, the librarian goes through every book (which represents websites). She quickly reads and makes notes (or indexes) about each book and where it can be found. Now, when someone comes and asks, "What's the best book on dinosaurs?" she doesn't just hand over the first dinosaur book she finds. She considers many things:

- Quality: Is the book well-written? Are the facts correct?
- Authority: Have other renowned authors or experts recommended or cited the book?
- Relevance: Does it closely match what the person is looking for?
- Recency: Is it a new book with the latest information, or is it a classic that has stood the test of time?
- Time of day: Maybe early in the morning, she recommends a light, kids-friendly dinosaur book, but later in the evening, she might suggest a detailed scientific one.

In the end, the librarian, using her method (or algorithm), offers a list of books that she believes best matches the person's request. That's how Google works, but it's sorting through websites instead of books!

Algorithm Bias

The unintentional discrimination arising from biased data or algorithm design requires awareness and mitigation to ensure fairness and inclusivity. Picture algorithms as chefs following recipes from a cookbook. If that cookbook only has recipes from one region, the chef might assume that's the only way to cook. Similarly, if an algorithm is trained only with data from one group or perspective, it might miss or misinterpret information from others. This unintentional oversight is called algorithm bias. Just as a diverse cookbook gives a fuller taste of world cuisines, algorithms need diverse data to make fair and inclusive decisions.

AI Governance

AI governance refers to the policies and guidelines for managing AI technologies within an organization. They address security, privacy, and compliance concerns. AI governance is like a rulebook for using AI in a company. It sets up rules to ensure AI is used safely, protects people's private information, and follows laws. Think of it as guidelines to ensure we use AI responsibly and not harm or misuse it.

Natural Language Processing

Natural language processing (NLP) is an exciting area because it allows machines to understand human language as people do. AI can understand, interpret, and respond to human language, enabling applications like chatbots, virtual assistants, and sentiment analysis.

A computer or robot can be programmed with rules on how to process words and sentences to interact with humans more naturally. For example, natural language processors allow computers to recognize a person's speech and respond with answers based on what it has learned. This means that instead of typing in commands, we can talk to our devices and they will be able to understand us.

This technology is essential because it makes us feel like we are communicating with another agent who can give us relevant information. When robots use natural language processing, they become more lifelike and better able to interact with humans meaningfully.

Neural Networks

Neural networks are a fascinating technology within artificial intelligence that small business owners should become familiar with. Neural networks are a type of machine-learning model that is inspired by the structure of the human brain. Essentially, an artificial neural network involves the creation of layers of connected "neurons" that can take in and process information, recognize patterns, and make predictions based on that information.

One of the critical differences between neural networks and other forms of machine learning is how the models are structured. Traditional machine-learning approaches often focus on creating algorithms to predict outcomes based on data inputs.

However, neural networks take a different approach by attempting to replicate the way our brains work. They do this by creating layers of artificial neurons that communicate with each other and adapt over time as they process new information.

Because of this unique approach, neural networks can do some truly incredible things. For example, they are used extensively in image recognition tasks, such as identifying faces or objects in photos. They can also be used in natural language processing, allowing machines to understand and interpret human speech and text in a way that was once thought impossible.

Deep Fake

Deep fake is a term used to describe videos, audio, and images manipulated by artificial intelligence to make them look genuine. In other words, it's a highly sophisticated way of creating fake content that is difficult to differentiate from the real one. These videos could make a person appear to say things they never said or make them do things they never did.

One of the biggest concerns with deep fake is that it could be used for malicious purposes, such as tarnishing the reputation of a business or an individual, spreading false information, or causing political unrest. As a small business owner, you must be aware of this threat to avoid being a victim of such fraud. It's essential to understand the difference between fake and reality so you're not misled into making crucial decisions based on false information.

Deep fakes are a growing concern as the technology behind them advances. The first step to keeping them out of the marketplace is to know what they are and where they come from.

IT'S GOING TO FEEL LIKE LEARNING A NEW LANGUAGE

Starting a business often feels like learning a new language, especially when you first encounter an accounting sheet. Suddenly, you're thrust into a world where terms like 'revenue' and 'profit' aren't just jargon but essential for the health of your business. Understanding these terms isn't just about keeping your business afloat; it's also about establishing your credibility as a business person. Just like grasping the nuances of a balance sheet, comprehending AI terminology is crucial in today's technology-driven business landscape.

When you talk about AI, you do so with confidence and understanding. Knowing the basic ideas and functions of the most common AI terms is akin to differentiating between assets and liabilities in accounting. This knowledge won't just prevent your head from spinning in conversations about AI; it will enable you to engage meaningfully and strategically.

The world of AI, much like accounting, comes with its own lexicon. It might seem daunting at first – but remember, you didn't learn the difference between gross income and net income overnight. Similarly, familiarizing yourself with AI terms is a gradual process, but it's one that will pay off. Understanding these concepts will demystify the technology and empower you to make informed decisions about how AI can enhance your business operations.

ONE FINAL ENCOURAGEMENT

Have you ever noticed how each generation seems to have its own technological 'comfort zone'?

Think about it.

Our grandparents, bless their hearts, often seemed bewildered by cell phones, treating them like alien artifacts rather than tools for communication. And our parents? Well, let's say their journey with social media has been... interesting. Some of us might secretly wish they'd resisted the lure of Facebook and Twitter, sparing us the occasional cringe-worthy post that only a loving parent could share.

Here we stand, facing our own technological crossroads with artificial intelligence (AI). Isn't it tempting to stay snug in our tech comfort zone, where everything is familiar and uncomplicated? But, as history shows, resisting technological evolution can be like trying to hold back the tide with a broom. It's not only futile but also a bit silly.

Let's not fall into the same trap as our predecessors. Embracing AI might feel daunting, but remember, once upon a time, so did using a smartphone or creating a social media profile. The cost of avoiding AI isn't just missing out on the latest tech trend; it's potentially lagging in a world rapidly embracing these new tools. And let's face it, nobody wants to ask when its too late, 'How does this AI thing work?' while everyone else already uses it to enhance their businesses and daily lives.

While it's comfortable to stick with what we know, let's nudge ourselves to understand the realm of AI. That may mean revisiting this chapter a few times until you understand the concepts a little better.

After all, we wouldn't want our future grandkids gently teasing us about being the most 'AI-challenged' generation, would we?

PART TWO
AI INTEGRATION AND MANAGING CHANGE

4 OVERCOMING AI IMPLEMENTATION HURDLES

L et's imagine that after months of speculating and planning, you decide to incorporate AI into your business. The promise of operational efficiency, enhanced customer experience, and a competitive edge has drawn you in. But as you begin the implementation stage, you're met with a bunch of unforeseen challenges. Integrating AI isn't like planting a seed and watching it grow; it's like trying to cultivate a delicate orchid in a constantly changing climate.

Your employees could be apprehensive, some even flat-out resistant. They could be fearful of potential job losses or worried about adapting to the new technology. You're also inundated with technical jargon from AI vendors, each claiming their tool is the "best." Deciphering which one genuinely aligns with your business needs feels like decoding a foreign language.

And then there's the time investment. Days become weeks, weeks turn into months. Every glitch, every setback, feels like a punch in the gut. The cost begins to creep up too. What was supposed to be a strategic investment now feels like a draining money pit. The anticipation of a seamless transition is replaced with sleepless nights, as you ponder whether you've made a costly mistake. The vision of AI propelling your business forward now seems clouded by the complexities of its integration.

This pain, this confusion, is what some small business owners could face during the AI implementation phase. But what if there were a roadmap, a guide to help navigate this path? The subsequent chapters aim to be that guiding light, ensuring you don't just survive the AI transition, but truly thrive in it.

Part 2 of this book aims to provide a comprehensive guide on the seamless integration of AI into your business operations. Starting with the core principles, we explore the foundational values essential for any AI integration, helping you align your business ethos with the evolving technology. With a myriad of AI tools available, choosing the right ones is overwhelming. I break down the process to ensure you make informed decisions that best serve your needs.

We do so always with your end result, the delight of your customers, in mind. We'll uncover the nuances of developing customer-oriented AI systems that enhance user experiences. We also want to keep everyone on board. As we navigate this transition, it's crucial to have a team that's both able and adaptable. But what happens when your current team's skills no longer align with your new trajectory? We also tackle the tough decisions, guiding you on when and how to revamp your team for the AI era.

A HELPFUL METAPHOR

I've benefited from the "Brilliant Intern" metaphor to help me see AI's role on my team at Get Clear, one of the companies I own. Imagine AI as your brilliant intern, a resource with potential and capability. Like a real-life intern, AI can help out with some of the things you don't want to do. But it's not just any intern, it's a brilliant one". The intern can comprehend many tasks (at once) and work with any information you throw at it. It can process data, analyze trends, and generate insights at an incredible speed, making it a valuable addition to your small business team.

Like a good intern, AI can handle repetitive and time-consuming tasks precisely. This frees up your valuable time to focus on other things. This delegation of routine responsibilities to AI allows you to operate more efficiently and strategically, just as a reliable intern lightens your workload.

We must note that the AI is still an intern. You don't give it everything. Setting boundaries and expectations is essential. AI's capabilities are not boundless, and it excels most when you provide clear guidance on what tasks it should handle and what still requires a personal touch. The collaborative synergy between your expertise and AI's analytical power unleashes your small business's full potential for growth.

My Experience With My Brilliant AI Intern

Allow me to share an account of how I've harnessed the power of AI, my brilliant intern, to help me everyday.

My brilliant intern, the AI, has become my go-to assistant. It's accessible through every device, laptop, phone, or tablet. If I'm running behind on a content delivery deadline (as always), I provide the AI with a topic, and it would generate compelling drafts for videos, social media posts, and blog posts. This saved me valuable time and ensured a consistent stream of high-quality content.

One of the standout features of my AI intern is its ability to decipher and summarize intricate technical communication. It drafts emails and proposals, even contracts for me (which my lawyer reviews). As the owner of a software company, I often receive updates and reports from our developers laden with technical jargon that perplexed me. I would pass these documents on to my AI intern, and within moments, it would translate and summarize the information in a way that I could easily understand. This kept me in the loop and empowered me to make informed decisions.

The brilliance of this AI intern is that it never says no to a task. Whether I need content for marketing campaigns, assistance with data analysis, or even a creative spark for brainstorming sessions, it's always at my disposal, working tirelessly 24/7.

My AI intern has become an indispensable asset to my business, embodying the spirit of a brilliant intern while offering unmatched efficiency, consistency, and availability. It's a true testament to the transformative potential of AI in today's business landscape, enabling me to navigate complexities, stay productive, and drive growth with unparalleled ease.

Viewing AI as your brilliant intern offers a fresh perspective on its role within your business.

Now, of course, it should be said as a reminder that AI is not really an intern nor a human. But the metaphor is helpful to personify it. We all know what an intern is and the role they can fulfill at a company. It just helps that they are brilliant and can do almost anything.

It's important to remember that AI, like an intern, is not a replacement for you or your unique expertise. Just as you wouldn't immediately place an intern in the most complex situations or expect them to handle customer interactions without training or supervision, you shouldn't throw a task at AI without looking over the output.

When nurtured, trained, and integrated effectively, AI can be a valuable asset, enhancing productivity, decision-making, and competitiveness in today's ever-evolving business landscape. As you guide and mentor your intern, you can cultivate and optimize AI's capabilities to help your small business flourish. Embrace this partnership, and you'll unlock the remarkable growth potential that AI offers to entrepreneurs and small business owners.

But It's Even Better

AI surpasses the brilliant intern in several crucial aspects, making it an invaluable asset for small business owners. Here are some examples of how AI excels:

1. 24/7 Availability: AI never sleeps or takes breaks. Unlike a human intern, AI is always operational, continuously monitoring data, responding to inquiries, and performing tasks outside regular business hours. This ensures that your business can provide instant support and access information around the clock, enhancing customer service and efficiency.

2. Consistency: AI delivers consistent performance every time. Human interns may have off days or variations in their work quality, but AI consistently executes tasks with precision and accuracy, reducing errors and maintaining high-quality output.

3. Instant Scalability: AI can effortlessly scale its capabilities to handle increased workloads. Whether you have a sudden surge in website traffic, customer inquiries, or data analysis requirements, AI adapts instantly to meet the demands, ensuring your business remains responsive and agile.

4. Processing Speed: AI processes data and performs calculations at unparalleled speeds. It can analyze vast datasets and generate insights in seconds, a task that would be overwhelming and time-consuming for a human intern. This speed lets you make real-time decisions and respond swiftly to market changes.

5. Multitasking: AI excels at multitasking, seamlessly handling multiple tasks simultaneously without losing efficiency. It can monitor social media channels, respond to customer inquiries, analyze website traffic, and perform various other functions simultaneously, which would be overwhelming for a human intern.

6. Data Analysis: AI can process and analyze vast amounts of data to uncover insights and trends that might go unnoticed by human analysis. It can identify patterns, anomalies, and opportunities, empowering data-informed decision-making.

7. Efficiency and Cost Savings: AI-driven automation reduces operational costs and enhances efficiency. It can handle repetitive, time-consuming tasks, allowing you to allocate resources and focus on value-added activities strategically.

8. Language and Translation: The right AI tool can communicate fluently in multiple languages and translate content in real time. This capability is ideal for businesses operating in global markets or providing multilingual customer support.

In these ways and more, AI not only complements but surpasses a brilliant intern's capabilities. While an intern brings a unique human touch, AI offers unmatched speed, scalability, consistency, and efficiency, making it an indispensable tool for small business owners aiming to thrive in today's competitive and fast-paced business environment.

By treating AI as a valuable team member and following this structured approach, you can maximize its contribution while minimizing disruption, ultimately enabling your business to thrive in the digital age.

Let's ensure that the integration of AI into your business is not only strategic and necessary, but also effective.

5 VALUES ARE THE FOUNDATION OF AI INTEGRATION

David, my entrepreneurial-inclined neighbor, and I have loved chatting over the years and over the fence about all things life and business. One day, he surprised me by revealing that he had recently purchased a well-known family-run butcher shop in town. That's the kind of random news you can expect when two entrepreneurs get together. I love this stuff and the ideas were flying right away.

The business he was purchasing had struggled as of late. He noted in his market assessment a tremendous opportunity to grow if things were done better. The shop had been a cornerstone of the community for decades. We both agreed that the traditional meat shop on the corner could once again thrive in the 21st century with the right improvements. Enthusiastic and tech-minded, David believed that he needed to integrate new technology to keep the business thriving in modern times.

What was more cutting-edge than AI?

Flush with ideas, he spent handsomely on several AI-powered tools he saw at a trade show:

- he started creating social media posts using a content generator
- that same software enabled him to write a regular newsletter in minutes, keeping front of mind with his customers
- he edited his videos in minutes using AI editing software
- an automated meat-cutting machine, promising precision like never before
- a chatbot for online meat orders to guide customers through their purchases.
- an AI-driven inventory system meant to predict the meat cuts and quantities he should be ordering based on trends and local events

Excitedly, David re-launched his new AI-empowered butcher shop. Not all was ideal at first. It didn't take long for issues to start surfacing. The AI-driven meat-cutting technology, while impressively precise, failed to capture the art of butchery. The steaks were uniformly cut but lacked the artisanal touch that many of his loyal customers appreciated. Some cuts of meat were too lean, missing those little pockets of fat that added flavor. Others seemed almost too perfect, missing the rugged charm of hand-cut meat. It created a lot of waste and some unhappy customers.

In an age when staff time was at a premium (and good people were in short supply), the chatbot for online orders initially seemed promising. Gone were the hours spent on the phone taking orders. This would be replaced by convenient online purchases. The shop and its clientele were ill-equipped to handle the nuanced questions of customers. One customer wanted to know the best cut for a slow-cooked stew, and the bot provided a generic answer, leading the customer to purchase the wrong meat entirely.

But the most jarring problem arose from the AI-driven inventory system. It began overstocking certain meats based on minor local events, leading to waste. On the other hand, popular items like prime rib or sirloin steaks often ran out during weekend rushes, as the system needed to account for human unpredictability and local preferences.

Within weeks, the ambiance of the once-beloved butcher shop changed. Customers missed the personal recommendations from the butcher, the hand-carved precision, and the familiarity of a shop that knew its community well.

Thankfully, small business owners have the flexibility to make swift adjustments. Realizing his miscalculations, David decided to reassess his approach. He recognized that while AI held promise, it couldn't replace the intricate knowledge and touch of a seasoned butcher or the human connection many sought when they visited.

Until the technology improved, he reverted to manual meat-cutting, retaining the traditional charm of the shop. They took some more time to train the AI inventory system. It needed more customizing based on his understanding of the business and its clientele. The chatbot was also tweaked to handle basic queries. It still took orders after business hours, but during the day, it directed customers to speak directly with the staff for requests.

In the end, the butcher shop regained its lost charm and customer trust. The experience taught David a crucial lesson: while AI can be a valuable ally, it is essential to weave it into the fabric of the business judiciously, always keeping the core values and customer needs in focus.

HOW TO START THE AI INTEGRATION PROCESS

After learning the basics of AI technologies, the next step is deciding which AI systems you should use. As David learned, you don't need to do everything all at once. With many steps in AI integration, selecting and integrating the right AI tools for your small business is a process that takes discernment.

But don't worry, I'll break down this seemingly intimidating task into actionable steps to ensure you select the best technology to suit your business needs and budget.

As we will discuss, it is important to regularly evaluate your business processes and determine where AI can have a positive impact. The first steps ask you to assess your values, current workflow, budget, and desired outcomes to find the most appropriate AI tools for your needs.

From there, it is possible to identify areas for improvement and measure the effect that incorporating AI could have on those processes —as well as weigh the potential cost against any potential rewards that might come from using such technology.

1. Define Your Values

The journey of AI integration begins with introspection. Understanding your values—as an individual and as a business—is paramount because they serve as a guide to making ethical and responsible decisions throughout the integration process.

As with any major shift in business, you must be clear and consistent with what you hold dear and ensure that AI aligns with those principles, never compromising your values or those of your customers.

Additionally, this new business world has given new meanings to the values most businesses claim to hold. With AI in the picture, a company's dedication to honesty might now include being honest about using AI tools or producing content using AI applications. We will discuss this further in the book.

New Values

Along with your typical cornerstone business values, such as loyalty, respect, and honesty, you will also need to determine your principles regarding AI implementation. As we discussed in Part 1, AI has its limitations, so you'll need to ensure that the AI applications you choose—and their integration into your small business—do not compromise on the basic level of service your customers have come to expect.

Let's consider this introspective, value-driven approach with an example of my neighbours butcher shop.

From its inception, the shop has been committed itself to fostering genuine human connections with its customers. It wasn't trying to compete with Big Box stores. The personality of a local butcher gave it a competitive edge. After learning to embrace AI's potential to enhance efficiency, the company employed AI-powered systems to streamline operations and improve service quality. However, they returned to their belief that the customer experience should always involve a human touch.

In line with this core value, David crafted a unique policy: They embraced AI but vowed that no customer would ever be left interacting solely with a robotic entity. Instead, AI was utilized as a support tool, empowering their staff with relevant insights and automating repetitive tasks behind the scenes. With online queries, the human support agent used AI to finish sentences, access templated response, and tap into data quicker than any manual process ever could. This approach not only upheld the company's commitment to human interaction but also proved to be a significant differentiator in a market dominated by impersonal automated systems.

By adhering to their values, David's butcher shop forged an unbreakable bond with their clientele. The human agents were quicker and more helpful than ever. As a result, the company flourished as 5-star reviews and referrals flooded in. This example showcases how successful integration of AI can be achieved while cherishing and preserving what matters most to us as individuals and businesses: authentic human connections.

As we venture into the realm of AI integration, David's story reminds us of the significance of aligning our actions with our values. Just like this local butcher, we too must be clear on our organizational values and craft a well-defined philosophy for how we will embrace AI and its interactions with our customers.

By remaining steadfast in our commitment to preserving what makes our businesses unique and valuable—genuine human connections, empathy, and personalized service—we can harness the power of AI while upholding our core principles.

Through thoughtful consideration and strategic planning, we can navigate the AI landscape with confidence, embarking on a journey that amplifies our strengths and propels our businesses into a future defined by collaboration between humans and technology.

Let's quickly work through an exercise that will give you clarity about your values as a company and how it will affect AI integration.

AI INTEGRATION VALUES ASSESSMENT

Question 1: What are your core values?

This question helps you identify and define the fundamental principles and ideals that matter most to you and your business.

Question 2: How might AI impact your core values?

Consider the potential effects of AI integration on your core values, both positive and negative.

Question 3: Are there new values specific to AI integration you must consider now?

Recognize the emergence of values related to technology and automation that may become important, such as 'ethical AI' or 'customer data privacy.'

Question 4: Can you create a clear AI philosophy aligned with your values?

Develop a concise philosophy or set of principles that reflect your commitment to integrating AI while preserving your core values.

Question 5: What is your strategy for AI integration while maintaining your values?

Outline a strategy for how AI will be integrated into your business processes and customer interactions while staying true to your core values.

Question 6: How will you communicate and implement these values across your organization?

Ensure that your values and AI philosophy are consistently communicated to your team and customers, so everyone understands your commitment to ethical AI usage.

2. Track All Your Systems

Tracking all your processes and systems refers to the practice of analyzing all the tasks that are performed within a business. This involves identifying which activities can be automated with an AI tool. By doing so, businesses can determine which areas are repetitive and require manual intervention, leading to inefficiencies and time-consuming procedures.

To identify these areas of opportunity, businesses must carefully analyze their current processes and systems. This includes considering how tasks are currently being performed, the amount of time they take, and whether there are any bottlenecks or inefficiencies in the process. The benefits of tracking all your systems include identifying opportunities for automation, simplifying workflows, minimizing human error, and reducing the time spent on repetitive tasks.

By understanding this information, businesses can then develop a comprehensive plan to automate processes that will benefit from AI tools.

Let's run a quick exercise to track your systems so we can identify where the opportunity lies.

EXERCISE: IDENTIFYING AUTOMATION OPPORTUNITIES

Step 1: Analyze Your Current Processes

Review all tasks within your business to identify which can be automated with AI. Look for repetitive and time-consuming procedures.

Step 2: Assess Efficiency

Examine how tasks are currently performed, considering time requirements and potential bottlenecks or inefficiencies.

Step 3: Assess The Benefits of Tracking

Recognize the advantages, including automation opportunities,
streamlined workflows, error reduction, and time savings.

3. Assess the Potential Added Value of AI

Next, we are going to find the most lucrative areas of opportunity.

After determining your values and distinguishing the systems within
your business, the next step involves analyzing each step of the workflow to identify areas where automation *could add value*.

By estimating the time saved from automating different workflows,
businesses can make informed decisions about how much value an AI
program could provide.

You can calculate the amount of savings that an AI tool could provide
with the following formula:

Savings = (Time Saved per Task × Number of Tasks Automated) ×
Hourly Cost of Labor

In this equation:

- **Time Saved per Task** refers to the amount of time (in hours)
  that the AI tool saves on each individual task compared to
  manual execution.
- **Number of Tasks Automated** represents the total number of
  tasks that the AI tool automates.
- **Hourly Cost of Labor** denotes the average cost of labor per
  hour, which is typically based on the salaries or wages of
  employees involved in performing the tasks that the AI tool
  automates.

Let's create a hypothetical example using my neighbor David's butcher shop to illustrate how the savings formula works with AI integration. We'll use some realistic numbers and scenarios for this purpose.

David's butcher shop employs a few staff members who handle various tasks like inventory management, customer service, and order processing. David has been considering an AI tool to automate some of these tasks, specifically inventory management and order processing.

Assumptions:

Time Saved per Task:

- Before AI: Inventory management and order processing take about 2 hours per day.
- After AI: The AI tool reduces this to 30 minutes per day.
- Time Saved per Task = 1.5 hours (1 hour and 30 minutes)

Number of Tasks Automated:

- Inventory management and order processing are done daily, so let's assume 30 days a month.
- Number of Tasks Automated = 30 days × 2 tasks/day = 60 tasks/month

Hourly Cost of Labor:

- Average hourly wage for the staff = $15/hour

Calculation:

Now, let's calculate the savings using the provided formula:

Savings = (Time Saved per Task × Number of Tasks Automated) × Hourly Cost of Labor

= (1.5 hours × 60 tasks) × $15/hour

= 90 hours × $15/hour

= $1,350

Interpretation:

David's butcher shop could potentially save $1,350 per month by implementing the AI tool for inventory management and order processing. This shows the direct financial benefit of saving time on these tasks.

David would then need to compare this savings against the cost of the AI tool (both initial and ongoing costs) to determine the overall return on investment (ROI). If the savings outweigh the costs, it suggests that the AI tool is a financially sound decision for his business.

By quantifying the value of time saved, David can make an informed decision about whether or not to adopt the AI tool in his butcher shop.

If the savings outweigh the costs, it indicates a positive return on investment (ROI) and demonstrates the worthiness of adopting the AI tool.

Once you determine how much value an AI tool could add to your business, it's time to find the right tool for the job.

4. Find the Right Tools

In the process of integrating AI into a small business, knowing the right tools to use is a pivotal step that can make or break the success of the endeavor. We will discuss helpful AI tools in the following chapter, but here, I want to highlight that while AI offers many applications and platforms, small business owners must approach tool selection with a strategic mindset rather than an obsession with every shiny new offering.

The key to choosing the right tools lies in maximizing efficiency and optimizing resources. Not every AI tool will be relevant or beneficial to a specific business's needs, and blindly adopting numerous tools can lead to unnecessary complexity and increased costs. By identifying the areas where AI can have the most significant impact on their business operations, owners and their teams can make informed decisions on tool selection.

Conducting thorough research on available AI tools and understanding their functionalities, pricing models, and user experiences is critical. Seeking feedback from other businesses that have already integrated AI can provide valuable insights. Additionally, exploring case studies and success stories relevant to the business's industry can inspire ideas and inform decision-making.

The good news is that you don't have to break the bank in this step. Most tools offer a trial of two weeks to a month (and if you call in Support at the end of the trial, most of them will happily extend it for you). You don't want to get subscription happy. AI is supposed to be an investment, not a liability.

Additionally, other factors such as improved accuracy, enhanced productivity, and the potential for scalability and growth should also be considered when evaluating the overall value of the AI tool to the business. Proper cost-benefit analysis and understanding the long-term impact of the AI tool on the business are crucial in determining its worthiness.

You should carefully assess whether they require a ready-made AI application that addresses their immediate needs or an AI platform that allows for customization and scalability. This decision will depend on factors such as the business's size, budget, technical expertise, and long-term AI strategy.

Alternatively, if the right AI tool doesn't exist for a specific business need, building a custom solution may be the best approach. Engaging with AI developers or partnering with AI-focused companies can help design tailor-made applications that align perfectly with the business's goals.

In conclusion, the careful selection of AI tools is an essential aspect of integrating AI into a small business. Avoiding unnecessary obsessions and instead focusing on identifying relevant and effective tools will lead to better outcomes. Whether choosing pre-built AI applications or developing custom solutions through AI platforms, a well-informed and strategic approach ensures that small businesses harness AI's potential to drive growth, innovation, and success.

5. Experiment and Evaluate

Step five—the crown jewel of embracing and integrating AI—is the art of experimentation and evaluation. Small business owners embarking on this transformative journey must grant themselves and their teams a healthy dose of grace as they navigate uncharted waters.

The key is to determine what strategies are working seamlessly and then seek ways to enhance them further. Simultaneously, any approach that falls short of expectations should be fearlessly discarded or reimagined, recognizing that each trial carries invaluable lessons.

By fearlessly forging ahead, these visionary entrepreneurs outshine their reluctant competitors, secure in the knowledge that progress and innovation await those who dare to embrace the future. Through this dance of exploration and refinement, small business owners will uncover the true potential of AI, propelling their enterprises to the forefront of a new era of success. The bravery to experiment and the wisdom to learn will forge a path where AI and human ingenuity unite to redefine what it means to thrive in the modern business landscape.

A QUICK WORD OF WARNING

It's easy to see the advantages of using AI in customer service applications—it can help businesses deliver faster and more accurate responses, increase efficiency, and lower costs. However, as David my butcher neighbor learned the hard way, it is important to consider potential drawbacks before implementing an AI-driven solution. Before you replace everything with AI in customer service, consider that utilizing AI without human assistance may provide a less satisfactory experience for customers.

Utilizing AI in customer service without human assistance: AI technology has become increasingly popular as a way to automate customer service interactions, but there's an argument to be made that the absence of human touch and connection can end up providing a less satisfactory experience for customers.

- AI does not replace empathy: AI technology can help businesses deliver faster and more accurate responses. However, it can't necessarily offer the same level of emotional understanding and compassion that a human representative would.
- AI could cause delays in customer service: AI solutions are often used to manage large volumes of inquiries quickly and efficiently, but there is a risk that the implementation of new technologies may cause unexpected delays or problems that were not present prior.
- AI might not be the most cost-effective solution for customer service: AI technology does have the potential to automate and streamline customer service operations, but it could end up being more expensive than hiring additional employees.
- AI can't recognize subtle nuances or body language: Human customer service representatives can interpret nonverbal cues from customers and adapt their responses accordingly. AI technology is still limited in detecting subtle nuances in a conversation and providing an appropriate response.
- AI's impact on customer loyalty: Ultimately, customers might become less loyal if they feel that their experiences with automated customer service systems need to meet their expectations. They may decide that human customer service representatives will better understand what they seek and provide a more personable experience.

AI is poised to become an increasingly important tool for small business owners. By implementing artificial intelligence into their workflows, we can streamline operations, reduce costs, and enhance customer experiences. Whether it's through chatbots, predictive analytics, or other AI-powered tools, there are endless opportunities for small businesses to harness the power of this game-changing technology.

Yes, the future may be uncertain, but small businesses can position themselves to thrive in this exciting new era by staying ahead of industry trends, evaluating existing technology, and continually optimizing AI systems with quality assurance testing, usability reviews, and user research.

As we saw in David's story, AI isn't a one-size-fits-all technology that fixes every problem. Rather, it is another new tool we can implement as small business owners. Just like with any tool, we need to learn how to handle it appropriately. In the coming chapters, we will discuss some AI programs you can use as well as how to manage your team through this period of change. By embracing this power, we can unlock countless opportunities for growth and success and build more innovative, efficient, and customer-focused businesses than ever before.

6 CHOOSING THE RIGHT AI TOOLS

When Steve Jobs said that "technology is a bicycle of the mind," he meant that technology, like a bicycle, is a tool that can help amplify human capabilities, specifically the human mind. Just as a bicycle can help us travel faster and farther than we could on foot, technology can enhance our cognitive abilities and enable us to achieve things that we couldn't otherwise.

According to Jobs, computers are not ends in themselves but tools to help us achieve our goals more effectively and efficiently. He believed that when used correctly, technology could make us more creative, productive, and connected to the world around us. By processing vast amounts of information and connecting us to a vast network of people and resources, technology can help us access new levels of understanding and insight.

Steve Jobs saw technology not as a standalone entity but as an extension of ourselves; a tool that can help us achieve our goals and dreams more easily and quickly. By viewing technology as "a bicycle of the mind," he helped shift our perspective on the role of computing in our lives, paving the way for a new era of digital connectivity and innovation.

The bicycle has often been compared to the mind and seen as a symbol of freedom, independence, and mobility. Similarly, the computer can be considered a bicycle for the mind, an aid that elevates the human desire for action and inserts itself as a means to a desired end. Because of the iPhone, we no longer see the computer as a destination but as something always with us, ready to call up a map, recommend a restaurant, or even keep us entertained with a simple game.

The rise of mobile technology has not led to increased computer usage but rather to a computer being accessible in more places than ever before. It is no longer necessary to be tied down to a desk to achieve great things with a computer. Instead, the computer has become a tool that is always at our fingertips, allowing us to create music, write novels, communicate with friends, navigate through unknown cities, and find companionship.

Computers trained with AI are helping us achieve more than we ever thought possible.

CHOOSING THE BEST AI SOFTWARE AND SERVICES

When selecting the right AI solution for you, it is important to not just focus on the surface-level marketing but to look more deeply into how well the software and services work with your small business. Here are some factors to consider before choosing the AI software you want to invest in:

- Does the software align with your business values?
- Can the software provide a level of service that your customers have come to expect?
- Is it easy to use?
- Does your team see the value in the software?
- Is the new software compatible with your existing software?
- Will it make your work quicker and more convenient?

UNDERSTANDING THE CRUCIAL ROLE AI PLAYS IN BUSINESS SUCCESS

AI is no passing trend but rather an ever-evolving and increasingly powerful toolset that can provide businesses with many opportunities to grow and remain competitive in any industry. As more companies adopt advanced AI solutions, those who do not will be disadvantaged regarding customer service, streamlining processes, reducing costs, or reaching new audiences.

7 CUSTOMER-ORIENTED AI

Meet Charlie, the entrepreneur with a zest for innovation and a soft spot for old-school charm. Charlie ran a small marketing agency. He did things like writing, website design and social media services for small businesses in his town.

Like many of us, Charlie always on the lookout for the next big thing to make his operations smoother and more profitable. Yet, Charlie had a quirky skepticism about AI tools. He felt threatened by them so he ignored they hype. Charlie pictured AI as friendly robots trying a bit too hard to be human. He loved technology but also believed in the magic of the human touch, especially in an industry where the trust of a client meant more than a thousand automated emails.

After spending months in an internal tug-of-war about AI, Charlie gave in to innovation. He introduced AI tools into his business, half-expecting them to start a robotic uprising. To his amazement, these tools turned out to be more like helpful elves than emotionless androids. They zipped through tasks with a precision that left Charlie both stunned and slightly embarrassed for ever doubting them.

Suddenly, Charlie found himself with an abundance of time – a rare commodity in the entrepreneurial world. He started channeling his inner creative genius into crafting new customer engagement strategies and even began toying with the idea of tapping into markets that were once just dots on his business map. The AI tools weren't just tools; they were his springboard to creativity, his backstage crew making sure the show always went on smoothly.

Charlie's lightbulb moment came when he realized that AI wasn't about replacing the human element; it was about amplifying it. He found himself making decisions at the speed of light (or at least at the speed of a very fast algorithm) and reinvesting resources into areas that truly mattered – like personally thanking Mrs. Henderson for her loyalty or brainstorming the next big customer appreciation event.

In a twist fit for a feel-good movie, Charlie discovered that embracing AI allowed him to be more human in his business approach, not less. He could now focus on what he loved most – building genuine connections, and innovating.

THE PSYCHOLOGICAL POWER OF AI IN ENHANCING CUSTOMER EXPERIENCE

In his book "Alchemy," Rory Sutherland presents a compelling case for "psychological moonshots." These are shifts in perception, often achievable without large-scale logistical transformations, yet they produce monumental impacts on user experience. As Sutherland elegantly puts it, "It's easy to achieve massive improvements in perception at a fraction of the cost of equivalent improvements in reality."[1]

Take everyday software like Uber. It's AI being used by people all over the world, every moment. Uber sounds like it's just us and a driver but there is a lot of AI happening all the time. Take, for example, Uber's map interface. We may take this fundamental part of the app's user experience for granted. It leverages AI in various subtle yet transformative ways to enhance the rider's experience.

Here's how…

The most visible feature is the real-time tracking of the car. This doesn't just show a car's movement but uses predictive AI to estimate the car's arrival time. It accounts for real-world factors like traffic conditions, potential roadblocks, and even the habits of the driver. By allowing riders to visually track their ride as it approaches, the uncertainty and anxiety traditionally associated with waiting for a cab are dramatically reduced. Can you imagine not knowing how long it will take for your ride to get there? But that's what we all had to do in the age of the taxi! We just called and then waited...and waited...and waited. We still have to wait for an Uber ride to show up, but now thanks to AI, it doesn't seem nearly as long.

And there's still more that AI is doing. The algorithms (you remember that word from before right?) analyze enormous amounts of data to suggest the most efficient route for the driver. This ensures that the rider gets to their destination in the shortest possible time, factoring in current traffic patterns and historical data.

Using historical data and real-time traffic conditions, AI helps in predicting accurate ETAs. This is crucial for riders to plan their schedules and reduces the anxiety of uncertainty.

In essence, Uber's map is a manifestation of AI-driven user-centric design. By focusing on the rider's experience and reducing points of friction (like the anxiety of waiting without updates), Uber has transformed the traditional taxi-hailing experience into something more transparent, efficient, and user-friendly.

AI AND YOUR COMPANY'S CUSTOMER SERVICE

AI can help revolutionize customer service by providing businesses with optimized processes, smart automation systems, and predictive analytics.

By implementing automated chatbot technology, companies are able to offer 24/7 customer service and support that would otherwise be impossible due to staffing limitations. This helps businesses answer queries quickly and efficiently, allowing customers to get the answers they need without needing to wait for a call center employee or email response.

Implementing AI in customer service can be likened to having a skilled sous-chef in a bustling restaurant kitchen. Just as a sous-chef takes care of the prep work, ensuring that ingredients are ready and basic tasks are efficiently handled, AI tools manage routine customer inquiries and automate simple processes. This setup allows the head chef – in this case, the customer service professionals – to focus on crafting the more complex, nuanced dishes that require their expertise and personal touch.

In this kitchen, the AI-powered chatbots and automation tools are like the sous-chef who tirelessly preps the vegetables, organizes the kitchen, and ensures that the basics are flawlessly executed. Meanwhile, the customer service team, like the head chef, can then dedicate their time to personalizing customer interactions, solving complex issues, and adding the special 'seasoning' that makes the customer experience unique and memorable.

Just as a successful restaurant relies on both the sous-chef and the head chef working in harmony, effective customer service in the age of AI depends on a balance between automated efficiency and human empathy. The AI tools handle the groundwork, allowing the customer service team to shine in their roles as the creators of delightful customer experiences.

Speeding Up Mundane Tasks: Our Dream!

Intelligent automation systems enable companies to manage their customer service processes more effectively by speeding up mundane tasks such as data entry or managing tickets. This extra time can then be reinvested in providing better customer experience through improved user experiences, tailored product offerings, or personalized messages that make the customers feel valued.

Voice recognition technologies can enhance existing interactive voice response (IVR) systems with natural language processing capabilities to understand customer requests better and process them faster than a human could. Lastly, predictive analytics allows companies to anticipate problems before they arise, enabling them to take preventive measures, which helps build trust between customers and the company as well as strengthen relationships over time.

While AI can bring great efficiency to businesses and save them time, it should not be used as a substitute for human-to-human interactions. Instead, it should be used to free up more time so that customer service professionals can provide greater customer attention, bolstering relationships and creating the best possible customer experience. AI tools should be employed as support tools so that more valuable time will be available for meaningful customer engagements.

DO CUSTOMERS LIKE AI?

Just because the technology is available doesn't mean it is useful for us. Would people prefer to connect with humans when they need help or would they rather have access to a robot that is a tireless expert on how to solve their problem?

I'll be honest with you, I go back and forth with how I answer that.

Sometimes I don't care if I make a friend on the phone—I just want my problem solved. It's late. I know nobody is working and that all the humans in my part of the world are likely sleeping. But imagine I just hit a snag in my workflow and I need an answer right away; that's when I'll take a robot. Or, what if Stan, the new customer support hire for the company I need help from, picks up the phone when I call. Stan just finished his training and it seems like I know more about the product than he does—again, give me a robot twelve times out of ten.

No offense, Stan. I'm sure you're still a good guy.

There, you have a perfectly good use case for customers who want chatbots.

AI AND YOUR MARKETING

Businesses can use automated marketing campaigns to access customers with targeted messages at the right time and place. Furthermore, machine learning algorithms help personalize ads, analyze customer behavior, and identify potential opportunities such as untapped markets or gaps in customer service that may have otherwise gone unnoticed. This extra edge helps ensure that every dollar spent is being used most effectively.

In addition, data analysis and NLP technology enable businesses to gain insight into customer behavior and preferences as well as understand customer sentiment analysis, giving them the ability to tailor their offerings so they can meet their customers' needs more efficiently. AI-powered tools also allow for improved customer relations, offering tailored product experiences, creating loyalty programs, and responding quickly to customer feedback.

Ultimately, adding AI to your business's marketing strategies can increase customer engagement and improve the return on investment (ROI). AI enables businesses to make sound decisions with less overhead cost, giving them more time and energy for other tasks such as improving the customer experience.

HOW WILL YOU USE AI IN YOUR BUSINESS?

Every business now faces the challenge of deciding when to use AI in customer service and when it may be best to rely on human-powered customer support.

By understanding the pros and cons of AI for customer service, businesses can make informed decisions about whether this technology will benefit their service operations.

Ultimately, the goal of incorporating AI into customer service should be to improve customer satisfaction and loyalty. By understanding the limitations of AI technology and leveraging its potential to streamline operations and promptly provide accurate responses, businesses can achieve improved customer experiences and cost savings.

With the right implementation and adaptation, AI could create a new world of better-automated customer service, allowing business customers to quickly and easily get what they need.

1. Sutherland, R. (2019). *Alchemy: The dark art and curious science of creating magic in brands, business, and life*. William Morrow.

8 HOW YOU'LL ADAPT YOUR BUSINESS TO AI

The Wall Drug story deserves to be in the Business Hall of Fame when it comes to adapting on the fly to a fast-changing world.

Wall Drug, a pharmacy located in Wall, South Dakota, gained fame by using clever marketing tactics to draw traffic from the nearby Interstate 90. Before the interstate highway system, small businesses like Wall Drug thrived. It was all about location. They were set up along the main routes that people traveled. However, when the interstate system bypassed many small towns (as popularized in the movie *Cars*), a lot of these businesses struggled because they were no longer on the main route.

In 1931, a man named Ted Hustead purchased the drugstore in Wall. At the time, Wall was a small town of 231 people.

Ted Hustead and his wife Dorothy were struggling to keep their business afloat during the Great Depression, and Dorothy came up with the ingenious idea of advertising free ice water to travelers heading to the newly opened Mount Rushmore, about 60 miles to the west. This was during the hot summer months when travelers were in dire need of refreshments.

They put up signs along Route 16A, offering free ice water at Wall Drug. The response was overwhelming. Soon travelers were flocking to the drugstore for a cool drink and then stayed to shop. The offer of free ice water turned Wall Drug from a small-town pharmacy into a thriving tourist attraction.

Wall Drug began to advertise on highways nationwide, often in the form of roadside billboards, with phrases like "Have You Dug Wall Drug?" This unique marketing technique transformed Wall Drug into a must-visit roadside attraction, not just for the free ice water, but also for its extensive gift shop, western art museum, chapel, and 80-foot dinosaur statue.

Like interstate highways, AI and machine learning systems have the potential to radically change society and how we do business. But they also are a new potential source of customers and traffic to our business, as long as we learn to adapt to the changing world. The story of Wall Drug is a testament to the power of innovative thinking in business, and AI represents the next frontier of this innovation. By understanding and harnessing the potential of AI, small businesses like Wall Drug find unique ways to serve their customers and stand out in the market.

WHAT'S THE DIFFERENCE BETWEEN OPPORTUNITY AND THREAT?

While it diverted the smaller, immediate flow of customers away from many small towns like Wall, it also opened up a vast, more diverse stream of potential customers travelling longer distances. This new highway system connected regions and states, bringing many travellers from far and wide. For businesses like Wall Drug, the interstate posed both a threat and an unprecedented opportunity.

Ted Hustead understood that while channelling customers away from the town's main streets, the interstate was also routing a much larger traffic volume relatively close by. He saw the dual nature of this development – a challenge to the traditional way of doing business, yes, but also a chance to tap into a broader customer base. By offering something as simple yet essential as free ice water, Hustead turned what could have been a business-ending obstacle into a thriving opportunity, attracting travellers who might otherwise have bypassed Wall entirely.

This foresight to recognize the interstate as a threat and a gateway to a vast new pool of potential customers was key to Wall Drug's transformation. In the world of AI and machine learning, a similar perspective is crucial. Small businesses must look beyond these technologies' immediate challenges to see the more significant opportunities they bring in reaching and serving a more expansive, varied customer base. Like the interstate highways, AI systems connect businesses to a broader world, offering new avenues for growth and innovation if we can adapt and harness their potential.

BEST PRACTICES FOR STAYING AHEAD

Implementing AI tools into your business can be overwhelming.

With the ever-evolving landscape of technology, it's important to discern which tools will help you achieve your goals and which will distract or divert you from them.

Here are some tips on evaluating your business needs, choosing the best AI software and services, selecting the right vendors, deploying your tools quickly and accurately, testing performance regularly for improvement over time, and getting the technical support you may need.

1. Test Your Performance

Testing and measuring the effectiveness of a newly adopted AI tool is crucial for a small business owner to ensure it is adding value to their business. The following are some steps and metrics that can be used to evaluate the success of an AI tool:

Define clear objectives: Before implementing an AI tool, it's crucial to have clear goals in mind. What problem do you want this tool to solve?

What process is it designed to improve? Clear objectives allow for specific, measurable results.

Monitor key performance indicators (KPIs): Based on your objectives, identify relevant KPIs that will help you measure the tool's effectiveness. If your goal is to increase customer engagement, for example, you might track metrics like customer retention rates, session time, or conversion rates.

Track user adoption and satisfaction: Measure how easily and willingly your team adopts the AI tool. High adoption rates and positive feedback suggest that the tool is user-friendly and beneficial. If your team struggles with the tool or avoids using it, further training may be needed, or the tool might not be a good fit.

Measure efficiency gains: One of the primary reasons for adopting AI tools is to automate routine tasks and make processes more efficient. You can measure this by comparing the time taken to complete certain tasks before and after implementation or by evaluating the volume of work completed within a specific time frame.

Monitor financial impact: Look at the tool's impact on your bottom line. Has it helped you cut costs, increase revenue, or improve margins?

Conduct regular reviews: Don't just set it and forget it. Regularly review the tool's performance and make adjustments as necessary.

Solicit feedback: Encourage feedback from your team and your customers. They can provide valuable insights into the tool's effectiveness and areas for improvement.

Remember, the goal of AI is to make business operations more efficient and improve decision-making. Therefore, a successful AI tool should ultimately lead to better business outcomes in line with your strategic objectives.

You may not see instant results like some of my examples. But you're learning what works. Monitoring and refining your AI implementation should form part of an ongoing process to ensure optimal performance and maximum benefits for you and your business.

2. Get Support from Experts

When problems arise with AI implementations, turning to qualified professionals is a wise choice. You can follow them on social media for free or you can hire them as personalized coaches. We will see a growing number of experts flood the marketplace, offering to help small businesses to implement AI.

Experienced pros can assist in troubleshooting and provide guidance on how best to approach any issue. They bring a level of expertise that can be invaluable when it comes to understanding the complexities of artificial intelligence. Reaching out for help should never be viewed as undesirable; no business leader should ever feel alone when working with AI software or services.

The right support can help boost confidence, foster productivity, and reduce stress—all of which are integral components of successful AI implementation.

3. Fall Without Failing

It is natural to make mistakes and have doubts when starting with AI tools, but it is important to remember that the best decision you can make is to take action.

Even if it is not the perfect choice, having a plan of some kind—together with professional support—is far better than standing still.

The worst decision you can make is no decision at all—and if you give yourself grace over time, you will eventually discover the right solution for your company's AI needs.

EITHER WAY, YOU'RE MAKING A DECISION

In the quest to integrate AI into your business, it's crucial to heed a profound lyric from the great Geddy Lee:

'If you choose not to decide, you still have made a choice.'

This rings especially true in the dynamic world of artificial intelligence. Indecision or delay in embracing AI doesn't just hold your business in stasis; it actively steers you away from the myriad opportunities that AI offers.

So, as you stand at the crossroads of AI adoption, remember that not making a decision is, in itself, a decision with significant implications. Every moment of hesitation is a missed opportunity for enhancement and growth. The landscape of AI doesn't pause or wait – it evolves relentlessly. By embracing this reality and choosing to engage actively with AI, you position your business to harness the full spectrum of benefits AI brings.

Let Geddy Lee's insight be your guide: the power to decide is the power to shape your business's future. Choose to explore, choose to learn, and choose to grow with AI. In doing so, you're not just making a choice about technology; you're charting the course for your business's journey in an AI-driven world.

9 CRUSHING IT WITH CONTENT

Remember the old days of content marketing? It was a labor of love – and sometimes just labor. Writing, editing, re-editing, posting, then rushing back to make more edits. Crafting content was like preparing a five-course meal every day, often during weekends and evenings, when you'd rather be unwinding. Each piece of content was a time-consuming journey, from the spark of an idea to the final click of the 'Publish' button.

But here's the exciting twist in our modern tale: AI tools have revolutionized this process, turning what used to be a marathon into a sprint. It's like switching from painstakingly chopping vegetables by hand to having a top-notch food processor do it in seconds. The struggle of creating content – once a time-intensive task reserved for those elusive pockets of free time – has been transformed into a smooth, efficient, and even enjoyable process.

With the advent of AI, the game has changed.

I'll show you how to leverage these advancements to not only stay ahead in your industry but also reclaim those precious weekends and evenings.

Here's how to harness the power of AI in your content marketing:

1. The Social Media Advantage

We're living in the age of social media. These platforms are like town squares where people gather and chat. Share your insights here, and you become the person everyone listens to.

2. Being in the Right Place

It's not just about being loud; it's about being heard. Figure out where your audience hangs out online, be it LinkedIn, Instagram, or niche forums, and be active there.

3. Become the Answer

People have questions, and they're looking for solutions. Through content marketing, you can be the one with the answers. That way, they'll come to see you as the expert.

4. Being Generous with Your Knowledge

Sometimes, giving away some of your secrets for free can come back to you in the form of trust and loyalty. It's like giving a sample taste at an ice cream parlor; people will come back for the whole scoop.

5. The Magic of Video

There's something about seeing and hearing a person that builds a connection. Videos let your audience do just that. It could be a simple tutorial or a sneak peek into your daily routine; it makes you real to them.

In a nutshell, content marketing is about consistently being there for your audience. It's about showing up, sharing, and caring.

YOU DO THE THINKING, AI DOES THE HEAVY LIFTING

Most people reading this live with the guilt that they should be doing more on social media. The problem is that they're just not doing it. No matter how many podcasts you hear about it or webinar trainings you sign up for (or just watch the replay), if you haven't done it on your own yet, you likely won't start posting on your own now.

Unless, that is, you have the right help.

Have you ever thought about machines doing some of the work for you? To me, this is one of the greatest advantages of using AI in your business. In the world of marketing, it means understanding what your audience wants and then delivering it to them.

For instance, consider a Large Language Model like ChatGPT. Think of it as your friendly neighborhood writer who's always on the clock.

UNLOCKING CREATIVE POTENTIAL WITH AI: MY PERSONAL JOURNEY

In the past year, I've created more content than ever before. It's been a whirlwind of ideas, drafts, and published pieces - a prolific period that has far surpassed any of my previous years. Reflecting on this surge in productivity, I've realized that two key lessons with AI have been instrumental in this journey.

1. AI as a Way to Generate Ideas

Firstly, AI has become an invaluable source of inspiration. There are moments in every content creator's life when the well of ideas seems to run dry. It's in these moments that AI has been my secret weapon. Whenever I find myself hitting a creative block, AI tools have been a fountain of fresh ideas. They offer a multitude of perspectives and suggestions that I can tailor to fit my audience and my unique voice. It's like having a brainstorming partner who's always ready to throw in a new angle or a different twist, pushing my creativity to new heights.

2. Transforming Notes into Narratives

AI has been transformative in converting my myriad of half-baked notes into cohesive and eloquent prose. If you're anything like me, you've got a treasure trove of thoughts, ideas, and observations scattered across various digital notebooks, phone memos, or buried deep in hard drives. These rough gems of content, previously dormant, have found new life through AI. By feeding these notes into AI tools, what once were fragmented thoughts have been woven into beautiful narratives. It's like watching a skilled artisan take raw, unpolished materials and craft them into something both elegant and meaningful.

This process hasn't just been about efficiency; it's been a journey of rediscovery.

Ideas that I had once jotted down and forgotten are now front and center in my content strategy, thanks to the transformative power of AI. It's as if I've unearthed hidden gold from the depths of my digital archives, turning them into valuable assets for my audience to enjoy.

If I can do it, so can you. Now I'm going to show you how.

CREATING A YEAR OF CONTENT IN AN HOUR: THE SMALL BUSINESS OWNER'S GUIDE

Let me show you how I would leverage the power of an AI LLM to create a year of content in less than an hour.

- **State your ideal customer:** Before you start, tell ChatGPT about your business. This will give it some context for the kind of outputs you need. *Prompt example: "I'm the owner of a skincare clinic in Vancouver. Our ideal client is a stay-at-home mom in her 30s. She doesn't often take time for herself like she deserves."*
- **Identify your audience's pain points:** Know what problems your customers face that your business solves. *Prompt: "List common problems faced by [your audience, e.g., 'stay at home moms' in relation to their skin]."*
- **Monthly themes:** Segment your year into overarching monthly themes. *Prompt: "Provide 12 monthly content themes for a [your industry, e.g., 'homemade skincare'] business."*

- **Generate weekly blog post ideas:** For each monthly theme, come up with a weekly blog post idea. *Prompt: "For the theme 'natural skincare,' give me ten blog post topics."*

- **Newsletter ideas:** Curate monthly newsletters summarizing your blog posts, sharing exclusive tips, or offering special promotions. *Prompt: "Write a blog post about (Idea #1)."* Repeat that for every blog post idea it gave you that you like.

- **Social media posts:** Turn your blog content into digestible social media posts. *Prompt: "Condense the blog post 'benefits of natural skincare' into five catchy social media captions."*

- **Engage with questions:** Encourage engagement by posing questions related to your content. *Prompt: "List interactive questions related to natural skincare to boost social media engagement."*

- **Share testimonials and reviews:** Showcase real-life feedback and experiences. *Prompt: "Create a template for sharing customer testimonials for skincare products."*

- **Promotions and announcements:** Use AI to craft announcements for sales, new products, or events. *Prompt: "Draft an announcement for a summer sale on skincare products."*

- **Tips and tricks:** Share useful tidbits related to your industry. *Prompt: "Generate five skincare tips for summer."*

- **Personal touch:** Incorporate behind-the-scenes glimpses or personal stories. *Prompt: "Create a storyline of a day in the life of a skincare product creator."*

- **Schedule and automate:** Use scheduling tools to post the content when you think it is best.

- **Monitor and adjust:** Every quarter, look back at your content's performance. See what's working and adjust accordingly. *Prompt: "Provide key performance indicators to monitor for content marketing in the skincare industry."*

Once you have these pieces in place, using your LLM, you can rapidly generate vast amounts of quality content that is tailored to your audience. This approach will help you maintain a strong online presence throughout the year.

NAVIGATING THE AI CONTENT WAVE: STAYING UNIQUE IN AN OCEAN OF VOICES

In an era where AI tools have democratized content creation, a new concern emerges: with everyone able to generate content at an unprecedented rate, will it eventually lead to a saturation where content loses its value? While this is a valid concern, let's unpack why there's still a distinct place for your unique voice in this crowded space.

1. The Ever-Expanding Internet Universe

Firstly, it's crucial to acknowledge that the internet was already a vast expanse of content before AI stepped into the picture. What AI does is not so much about adding to the quantity but enhancing the quality and reach. The digital landscape is vast enough to accommodate the influx of AI-assisted content without diluting individual value. The key is not merely to contribute to the volume but to add depth and distinctiveness to your content.

2. The Reality of Execution

While it's true that AI tools are now more accessible, the act of consistently creating and executing a content strategy remains a challenge that many will not undertake. There's a vast difference between casually playing with AI tools and diligently using them to craft a sustained, engaging content narrative. The discipline, dedication, and strategic approach to content creation will set apart serious content creators from those merely riding the AI wave.

3. Your Unique Perspective: The Ingredient You Can't Replace

The most crucial aspect to remember is this: AI is a tool, not a replacement for your unique perspective. Your individuality, the way you see and interpret the world, is your most vital asset. AI can assist in bringing your vision to life but cannot replicate the essence of who you are. Adapt the outputs to fit your voice, infuse it with your insights, and use it to amplify, not overshadow, your unique way of looking at things.

Addressing the question of plagiarism, particularly in the context of using AI tools for content creation, is crucial. Plagiarism is the act of using someone else's work or ideas without proper attribution, and it's a serious ethical concern in any field, especially in writing and content creation.

When using AI tools like ChatGPT or other content generation software, the content produced is typically original in terms of not being a direct copy from an existing source. These tools generate responses based on a wide range of inputs and data they've been trained on, and they don't pull content verbatim from specific articles, books, or other media. However, this doesn't automatically exempt the output from plagiarism concerns.

One key aspect to consider is the source of the ideas and information fed into the AI. If the input is heavily based on specific, identifiable sources, the output might closely mirror those sources, raising potential plagiarism issues. In academic, professional, and creative contexts, the originality and expression of ideas are paramount. So, if the AI-generated content closely resembles the ideas, structure, or specific expressions found in existing works, it could be considered plagiarism if not correctly attributed.

It's also essential to consider the expectations and norms of the field in which you're working. For instance, academic writing has strict rules about originality and attribution, while content marketing and creative writing might allow more flexibility in using AI-generated text.

To avoid plagiarism when using AI tools:

1. Use AI for Ideation, Not Duplication: Leverage AI to generate ideas, outlines, or drafts, but ensure that the final content reflects your unique analysis, voice, and insights.

2. Check for Unintentional Similarities: Use plagiarism-checking tools to ensure that AI-generated content hasn't inadvertently replicated existing material.

3. Add Personal Insight: Infuse AI-generated content with your perspective, insights, and voice to make it your own.

4. Attribute Appropriately: If you use specific inputs or base your content on existing materials, provide proper attribution and references.

Embrace AI As You Embrace Yourself

While AI opens the floodgates to mass content production, it doesn't diminish the value of authentic, thoughtfully crafted content. Embrace AI to refine and express your ideas more effectively, but always let your individuality lead the way.

The goal is not to compete with AI in content quantity but to leverage its capabilities to enhance the quality and authenticity of what you share. Remember, in the vast world of content, there's only one you – and that's your ultimate advantage.

A TRANSFORMATIONAL SHIFT IN HOW CONTENT IS MADE

As we wrap up this chapter, it's clear that the integration of AI in content marketing is not just a trend; it's a transformational shift in how businesses engage with their audience. The journey we've embarked upon reveals the immense potential of AI to elevate our content strategy, making it more efficient, targeted, and impactful.

The days of toiling over content creation are fading into the past. With AI tools like ChatGPT, we've seen how the once-daunting task of generating a year's worth of content can now be accomplished in less than an hour. This newfound efficiency frees up your time and energy, allowing you to focus on what truly matters – connecting with your audience and growing your business.

But remember, while AI is a powerful ally, the human touch will continue to drive meaningful connections. The creativity, empathy, and understanding you bring to your content strategy will resonate with your audience. Use AI as a tool to enhance these qualities, not replace them.

As you go, keep experimenting with AI, measure the effectiveness of your content, and stay adaptable. Everything is constantly shifting with content marketing. Trends come and go. We need to move fast to keep up. Now, with AI as your co-pilot, you're well-equipped to navigate these changes and stay ahead of the curve.

The fusion of AI with your unique brand voice and insights paves the way for a new era of content marketing – one that's more dynamic, personalized, and engaging. So embrace this journey with optimism and creativity, and let's reshape the future of content marketing together.

10 MANAGING CHANGE WITH YOUR TEAM

Death, taxes, and change. Those are the three constants in our world. Small business owners will experience all three in the course of their lifetimes. Think of how much technology has changed in the past decades. Let's imagine how much a 90-year-old family-run company has evolved over the years. Don't get too caught up in the logistics. I only want to quickly highlight just how much and quickly things change.

Three generations have owned and operated the family business we are going to call Winston Vacuum Supply. While the last name has been consistent over decades in business, the family has had to adapt and evolve as technology changed the way they did business.

The first generation witnessed the emergence of electricity. This innovation revolutionized their workplace. They marvelled at how electric fans replaced hand-held ones, providing much-needed relief on hot summer days. Automatic cash registers simplified transactions, making it easier to manage sales and inventory. The most significant change, however, was the ability to light up the workplace after sundown, allowing them to work longer hours and boost their productivity.

As time passed, the second generation experienced the introduction of automobiles. This new mode of transportation enabled them to travel more quickly, expanding their reach beyond the small town and into neighboring cities. Their business flourished as they connected with new suppliers and customers, further driving their growth.

But the world didn't stop there. The aviation industry took off, opening up global markets for the third generation of entrepreneurs. They could now source materials from distant lands and sell their products to customers around the world. Their once small-town business had transformed into an international enterprise.

As the years went by, the family business was passed on to the fourth generation of entrepreneurs. That brings us to today. Just like their predecessors, they faced new challenges and opportunities brought about by technological advancements. The rise of the Internet had already transformed their business, but now they were confronted with another groundbreaking innovation: artificial intelligence.

The Winstons of modern day have realized the potential of AI and its ability to streamline operations, enhance customer experience, and optimize decision-making. They started by implementing AI-powered chatbots on their website, providing round-the-clock support and assistance to customers worldwide. This not only improved customer satisfaction but also freed up valuable time for the team to focus on more strategic tasks.

They also switched to AI-driven data analytics tools to better under-stand their customers' preferences and behaviors. This valuable insight allowed them to tailor their marketing strategies and product offerings, resulting in increased customer loyalty and revenue growth.

To stay ahead of their competition, they've adopted AI-powered supply chain management solutions. These systems helped them predict demand, optimize inventory levels, and reduce costs, ensuring their business remained efficient and profitable.

Understandably, these changes evoked initial skepticism from some members of the older generations. However, their willingness to adapt and innovate quickly demonstrated the undeniable benefits of AI, winning over even the most resistant skeptics.

Together, the family continued to evolve their business in the face of new technological advancements, maintaining their legacy of adaptation and resilience. The story of the Winston family business serves as a testament to the power of embracing change and harnessing the potential of AI, inspiring future generations to continue pushing the boundaries of innovation and growth.

LEADING THROUGH CHANGE

Introducing AI into a business is indeed a significant shift. This change can seem daunting and face resistance due to several reasons. Here are some of the key reasons why people often resist change:

1. Fear of the unknown. People naturally tend to be uncomfortable with uncertainty. When it comes to AI, many employees might not fully understand what it is and how it works, leading to fears about its impact on their roles or the business at large.

2. Job security. The introduction of AI often raises concerns about job security. Employees may worry that automation will render their roles obsolete, leading to layoffs.

3. Change in routine. People typically develop routines and processes over time that they are comfortable with. AI may disrupt these established ways of doing things, causing discomfort.

4. Lack of perceived benefits. If the benefits of AI are not clearly communicated or understood, employees may question why the change is necessary. They might not see the need for AI if they believe current systems and processes are working fine.

5. Poor communication and training. Without effective communication about why the change is happening, what it entails, and how it will affect everyone, resistance is likely. Additionally, without proper training and support, employees may feel ill-equipped to deal with the new systems brought by AI.

6. Distrust of leadership. In a world of shifting power dynamics and misinformation, one of the most powerful tools you can wield is building trust with your employees. Keeping your messaging clear, consistent, and in line with the established values of your company will help your employees stay calm as you guide them through periods of change.

Overcoming resistance to AI, or any significant change, requires clear communication, education, and patience. Leaders need to be empathetic, taking the time to understand their team's concerns and address them. Training sessions should be provided to help employees understand the new technology, how to use it, and how it can make their work easier or more efficient.

By focusing on these elements, business leaders can help their teams embrace AI and other changes, turning potential challenges into opportunities for growth and improvement. Like scaling a mountain, it's not an easy journey, but the view from the top—in the form of enhanced business performance and satisfied employees—makes it all worthwhile.

When you ensure everyone understands why these changes are being made and how they will positively impact everyone's lives in the long run, you can help your team embrace what may feel like a difficult transition initially. With a clear strategy and plenty of empathy and understanding, introducing AI into any organization can be done effectively and successfully, leading to happier staff and improved productivity in the end.

HOW TO DISCUSS AI WITH YOUR TEAM

Here are four of the principles that I've observed:

1. Address Concerns About Job Security

Explain how implementing AI technology won't lead to reduced roles or job losses but instead will augment existing skills and give staff opportunities to up skill and become even more valuable.

In today's age of expanding technology, there is no doubt that AI will play a bigger role in the future of work. But addressing the anxiety and insecurity surrounding introducing AI into business can be daunting— particularly regarding job security.

Rest assured, however, that if implemented properly, AI technology enhances existing skills and brings great opportunities for staff to upskill, making them even more valuable. It is not about replacing jobs with machines but rather augmenting them with the assistance provided by artificial intelligence to drive efficiencies and reduce costs —allowing staff to focus on complex problem-solving activities that make an impact.

Businesses need to make sure their teams are comfortable with this change before introducing advanced AI systems into the workplace— after all, success lies in embracing it together!

2. Highlight the Benefits of Implementing AI

Showcase how implementing artificial intelligence can benefit the team. For example, AI technology can help boost efficiency, reduce costs, and automate mundane tasks so that your team can focus on creative problem-solving activities that make an impact.

Using machine learning techniques with the help of AI systems also allows your team to gather actionable insights from data analysis and precision quickly. This means decisions can be made without wasting precious resources, leading to more success in the long run.

With the right tools in place to support staff in utilizing AI safely and securely, businesses can ensure they are taking advantage of this technology while still embracing human skill sets—it's all about getting the balance right!

3. Emphasize How AI Augments Human Skills

Explain how AI relies on human expertise to train data and make final decisions about actionable insights gathered from data analysis. Show them that with appropriate tools in place, staff can utilize machine learning techniques to their advantage with more precision than ever before, boosting their career prospects in the process.

With appropriate tools for staff to utilize machine learning techniques safely and securely, businesses can take advantage of this technology without losing valuable human skill sets.

The benefits of using AI go beyond cost reduction—it also allows employees to develop their skills in ways that weren't possible before. With more precision than ever, staff can make informed decisions quickly, allowing them to stay ahead of their competition and reduce the time needed to complete tasks.

Not only does this improve business effectiveness and boost career prospects, but it also instills confidence in staff as they understand how their individual decisions and expertise contribute towards a successful future.

4. Assure Them That Change Is Manageable

Reassure them that change doesn't have to be overwhelming but can be approached incrementally with clear objectives and achievable goals set out at each stage of development. Include practical tips for managing the transition period effectively, such as introducing new ideas gradually or providing refresher courses to ensure everyone is comfortable using the new technology before its deployment across teams.

Here are some practical tips for managing this transition period effectively:

1. Introduce new ideas gradually and in small steps. This will give staff the time and space to get used to the changes before they become commonplace.
2. Provide refresher courses so everyone is comfortable using the new technology before deploying it across teams.

3. Set clear objectives and achievable goals at each stage of development to ensure everyone knows what needs to be done and when it needs to be completed.
4. Establish a feedback system so that staff can provide feedback on how the changes work for them and make adjustments as necessary.
5. Celebrate successes along the way—recognizing even the smallest milestones will help keep your team motivated!

By following these steps, you'll ensure a smooth transition when introducing artificial intelligence into your workplace, boosting morale and productivity within your team.

SETTING A NEW STANDARD

Anyone can access the same tools and resources as experts in any field, but it takes a special skill and expertise to utilize them effectively.

This is even more true when it comes to AI technology. Just like anyone can buy ingredients from a grocery store and cook a meal, but only the most skilled chefs will be able to create a fine-dining experience. Similarly, anyone can purchase AI tools, but only those willing to put the work in to use AI properly will realize their full potential.

AI won't replace people; rather, people who don't have an understanding or mastery of AI may be replaced by other people who understand how to use these advanced technologies effectively.

Evaluate your business needs and goals with mindfulness, select suitable AI software and services carefully, make timely deployments, test performance often for improvement over time, and enlist professional expertise when needed.

All of this will help establish a strong foundation that can be built upon as your business progresses. Every step may not be perfect, and mistakes are inevitable. Don't be afraid to take risks and embrace failure as part of the learning process.

WHAT TO DO WHEN YOU REALIZE YOU NEED A NEW TEAM

While reading the last section, you might have realized that you need a new team (not uncommon for business owners – AI is certainly not the only catalyst for this type of thinking). What do you do when you realize the people you currently have on the company bus have not and will not embrace the new reality of a world with AI?

That will naturally lead us to another question: *How to use AI to do HR?*

This is not a book about putting together the right team. There are many books written on this topic. I want to give a use case for how you can use AI tools as a small business owner. Building your team more efficiently will be a welcome addition to your arsenal.

The good news is that AI is making finding the right people much easier.

The realm of Human Resources (HR) is undergoing a transformative shift, thanks to AI. The traditional hiring process, once characterized by manual resume screenings and time-consuming interviews, is now being augmented by AI's precision and efficiency.

Imagine a scenario where a small business owner, already juggling multiple roles, receives hundreds of applications for a new position. In the past, this would mean long hours sifting through resumes, trying to find the perfect fit. But with AI, this process is streamlined. Advanced algorithms can quickly scan through resumes, highlighting candidates that best match the job's requirements. But it's not just about speed; it's about making more informed decisions. These systems can predict a candidate's success in a given role based on their profile, ensuring that businesses get the right person for the job.

But the benefits of AI in HR aren't limited to the employers. Job seekers, too, are finding value in this technological evolution. There are now platforms that use AI to match candidates with suitable job opportunities, turning the often daunting task of job hunting into a more personalized and efficient experience. Some AI-driven tools even offer feedback on resumes, guiding applicants on how to present themselves better.

However, as with all powerful tools, there are considerations to bear in mind. The rise of "algorithmic creep" poses a challenge. This term refers to an over-reliance on algorithms, which, if not carefully managed, can lead to unintended consequences. For instance, if not correctly designed, these algorithms might inadvertently favor certain types of candidates over others, leading to biases in hiring. It's a reminder that while AI can be a valuable assistant, human judgment and oversight remain crucial.

There's also the broader question of what AI means for the future of jobs in HR. While certain tasks might become automated, it's essential to recognize that new roles and opportunities often emerge in tandem. For small businesses, this might mean a shift in focus, with HR professionals spending less time on routine tasks and more on strategic planning and employee engagement.

As AI continues to weave its way into the fabric of HR, small businesses stand at the threshold of a new era. An era where hiring is not just faster but smarter, where businesses can find the right talent with precision, and where job seekers are matched with roles that truly resonate with their skills and aspirations. As with all technological advancements, the key lies in balanced adoption, ensuring that while we harness AI's power, we also remain attuned to its challenges.

When You Have To Let Someone Go

This is a book about AI and not an HR manual. That being said, I am a small business owner who has had to have tough conversations with employees and let them go. I haven't always done it well but I certainly have learned.

Releasing an employee from their duties is a task that requires a delicate balance of empathy, clarity, and firmness. It's a moment that can be fraught with emotion and uncertainty, both for you as a business owner and the employee. However, when approached with care and understanding, it can be managed in a way that respects the dignity of the individual and the needs of your business.

First and foremost, it's essential to recognize that letting an employee go is never an easy decision. Still, sometimes, it's necessary for the health and evolution of your business, especially in an era where adapting to new technologies like AI is crucial. When you realize that an employee's skills or mindset no longer align with the direction your business is heading, it's a challenging but essential realization.

In preparing for this conversation, planning your approach thoughtfully is vital. Ensure the meeting is in a private, comfortable space where the discussion can be conducted without interruptions. Be direct yet sensitive in your communication. Clearly explain the reasons for the decision, focusing on the business's needs and future direction rather than personal shortcomings. It's crucial to convey that this decision isn't made lightly and that you've considered all other options.

Acknowledge the contributions the employee has made to your company. Showing gratitude for their efforts can help maintain their dignity and soften the blow of the news. It's also important to listen to them, allowing them to express their feelings and thoughts. This conversation is not just about conveying a decision; it's also about providing closure.

Offer support in their transition through a reference letter, guidance on their next steps, or assistance in finding new opportunities. This gesture of support demonstrates that your concern for their well-being extends beyond their tenure at your company.

Finally, consider the impact of this decision on the rest of your team. Be prepared to address any questions or concerns they may have in a way that respects the privacy of the individual leaving while also reaffirming your commitment to the team and the future of the business.

In conclusion, releasing an employee is a complex process that needs to be handled with the utmost professionalism and compassion. It's about making a decision that, while challenging, is in the best interest of both the individual and the business. You can ensure a respectful and constructive transition for everyone involved by approaching this situation with empathy and a clear rationale.

INTEGRATING AI: A FINAL NOTE

Figuring out how to thrive in the world of AI for a small business can seem daunting. The rewards are vast for those who persevere. It's about steering the ship through stormy seas toward clearer horizons.

What we learned in this section:

- Grounding decisions in our core values makes AI integration meaningful and purposeful.
- Prioritizing customer experience is key. AI should enhance, not replace, genuine interaction.
- Adaptability is crucial as AI continues to evolve.
- Content strategy, enhanced by AI, can greatly boost visibility and engagement.
- Teams will evolve, but open communication ensures that changes lead to growth rather than discord.
- At times, a team reshuffle might be necessary for innovation.

Remember, while AI is a powerful tool, your entrepreneurial spirit is the driving force. Harness the potential of AI and let it be a wind in your sails.

PART THREE
ETHICAL AI USE

WHEN PROGRESS BRINGS UP THE CHALLENGES OF POWER AND RESPONSIBILITY

We're in the middle of a technological wave that represents a monumental shift in human history. It promises unprecedented advancements and benefits that will transform our healthcare systems, grow businesses, and launch industries we haven't even conceived of.

However, as Uncle Ben once taught young Peter Parker (Spiderman) taught us, "with great power comes great responsibility." The rapid spread of these technologies carries an inherent risk. If misused or misunderstood, the very tools intended to propel us forward could inadvertently set us back or, worse, harm us. This dilemma, where we grapple with the balancing act of harnessing versus controlling technology, is what Mustafa Suleyman, an AI expert and author of *The Coming Wave*, calls the "containment problem."[1] He argues that we face a historical problem of not just about unleashing technological potential, but also ensuring that we have the necessary safeguards in place to avoid unintended negative consequences.

A stark example of this issue can be seen in the case of *Cambridge Analytica*, once a prominent player in the field of political consulting. The company became the epicenter of a controversy that rocked the foundations of data privacy. Through the guise of an innocuous Facebook quiz, the firm harvested data from 87 million users, most unaware of the intrusion.

With this vast dataset, they sculpted psychological profiles to sway minds during pivotal moments like the 2016 U.S. Presidential Election.

As the curtain of their operations was pulled back by journalists and whistleblowers, a global uproar ensued. Facebook faced a reckoning for its loose data gates, while Cambridge Analytica crumbled under scrutiny.

This scandal spotlighted the perilous dance between data, ethics, and democracy, prompting a worldwide push for stricter data protection.

CAN ETHICS KEEP UP WITH AI?

In just a few short years, AI has undergone breathtaking advancements. It's no longer just a tool for complex calculations.

Today's AI can write, craft visuals, manage complex logistics, and even help medical professionals diagnose rare diseases. What's even more astounding is the sheer scale and speed of AI's growth. Its capabilities have expanded exponentially, and its integration into everyday consumer tech is more rapid than anything we've previously witnessed. As we stand on the brink of this new era, it's paramount that small business leaders approach the potential of AI with both enthusiasm and caution.

---

1. Suleyman, M. (2023). *The Coming Wave*.

11 NAVIGATING THROUGH THE ETHICAL AGE OF AI

A I has emerged as a potent force, evoking a mixture of awe, apprehension, and contemplation. The underlying threat perceived by many isn't merely hypothetical; its ability to usher in catastrophe is imminent. We focus our attention here not on the global ethical issues of AI but rather on how they affect your business.

To understand the shift into the age of AI, one must evaluate the cost to humans. We as a species, while ingenious and adaptable, come with a price tag. With an average annual expense of $60k, the financial burden they represent for employers is clear. Moreover, the human psyche, with its intricate web of emotions and vulnerabilities, can sometimes be its own worst enemy. Feelings of depression, overwhelming stress, and occasional lethargy can hinder consistent productivity. And when pitted against machines in terms of raw efficiency, such as basic calculations, humans are undeniably slower.

However, I believe it's a fallacy to see AI as the quintessential threat. The real challenge lies not within the algorithms but in our response to them. The heart of the matter is human discretion. Armed with the power of AI, will we make informed, ethical decisions? Or will we err, driven by shortsightedness or greed? The real dialogue isn't about AI usurping humanity but about humans wielding AI responsibly. It's an introspection of our values, our choices, and, ultimately, our vision for the future.

A NEW ADVENTURE IN ETHICS

Embracing AI is like stepping into a new, exciting adventure. It's full of promises like making work easier, faster, and smarter. But as you take this journey, you come across a big problem—the question of what's right and wrong when using AI.

Each new technological stride in AI comes tethered with ethical knots —questions of privacy, transparency, accountability, and bias that aren't merely philosophical musings but pressing concerns that impact real lives.

ETHICAL ISSUES WE WON'T BE TALKING ABOUT

While this chapter explores the ethical dimensions of AI specifically for small businesses, it's worth noting that the broader discourse on AI ethics spans a wide array of topics, many of which are beyond the scope of our current discussion. For instance, international law grapples with questions about AI's role in warfare, surveillance, and cross-border data sharing. There's also the intriguing yet controversial concept of a social credit system, where AI plays a pivotal role in monitoring and scoring citizens based on their behavior and interactions. On the frontier of scientific innovation, projects like Neurolink aim to merge the human brain with AI, raising profound ethical questions about identity, privacy, and the very nature of human experience. And then there's the realm of AGI (*Artificial General Intelligence* - you'll remember that's the scary one) – the hypothetical AI that possesses intelligence comparable to human capabilities, with its own set of philosophical and ethical quandaries.

However, as small business owners, our immediate concerns with AI ethics might be more grounded, focusing on its day-to-day applications in our operations, customer interactions, and decision-making processes. It's about ensuring fairness in AI-driven hiring practices, transparency in customer recommendations, and accountability in automated decision-making.

By narrowing our focus in this chapter, we aim to provide actionable insights and guidance tailored to the unique challenges and opportunities that small businesses face in their AI journey. While the broader ethical debates around AI are undoubtedly fascinating and crucial, our goal here is to equip you, the small business owner, with the knowledge and tools to navigate the immediate ethical landscape of AI in your business operations.

IT'S ONLY GOING TO INCREASE

As AI's capabilities amplify, so do its ethical quandaries, stirring up a whirlwind of issues we must confront. Here are a few we wrestle with today and more in the future:

- When machines start making decisions, who is held accountable when things go wrong?
- When algorithms sift through mountains of data, who ensures they don't perpetuate harmful biases or invade personal privacy?
- How do we prevent these intelligent systems from becoming black boxes whose workings are unfathomable, even to their creators?

You'll need to start developing your own views and values on these topics. You don't want to be caught off guard with ethical situations. Like all matters in running a small business, you want to be prepared for them.

SEIZE THE OPPORTUNITY TO BE VIRTUOUS

As business leaders, we can seize this opportunity to showcase ethical leadership, making a conscious commitment to create a work environ-

ment that values human well-being and nurtures growth and empowerment. By upholding the dignity of our workforce and treating our
employees and customers with respect and empathy, we can illuminate
a path toward a future where AI and human potential harmoniously
coexist.

Rather than waiting for governmental regulations, we should embrace
this responsibility now, embodying the values of integrity and compassion in every decision we make.

WHAT IS ETHICS ALL ABOUT?

Ethics is the philosophical study of human behavior, specifically in
society. It is concerned with developing a moral framework to guide us
in personal and professional contexts. Ethics involves examining the
principles and values that underpin our beliefs and actions and evaluating them based on their moral worth.

Ethics is important because it helps individuals develop a sense of
right and wrong. It promotes empathy, compassion, and respect for
others. Ethical behavior ensures that individuals, groups, and organizations act in a responsible and accountable manner toward others,
society, and the environment. It ensures that complex societal problems
are addressed in a fair and equitable manner and that decisions are
made with the best interests of all in mind.

WHY DO WE NEED ETHICS IN AI?

In today's fast-paced technological landscape, the role of AI is
expanding rapidly, touching virtually every aspect of our lives. As AI
continues to evolve and integrate more deeply into various industries,
the importance of ethics in AI becomes increasingly evident. Small
business owners, like their counterparts in larger organizations, need
to ensure that ethical considerations are integral to deploying AI tools
in their businesses.

At its core, the need for ethics in AI revolves around the principle of
"doing no harm."[1] AI systems can impact a broad range of areas,

including privacy, data security, employment, and even the psychological well-being of individuals. These are sensitive areas for most of us who depend on these working for us to flourish. AI should add to our lives, not damage them.

AI can also perpetuate societal biases embedded in their training data, leading to discriminatory practices. Therefore, it's vital for small business owners to understand these potential risks and to work towards minimizing harm. Previously, I mentioned how AI could be used to do HR more efficiently. But it should be done with unbiased software. One example of AI perpetuating societal biases, particularly in small businesses, occurs within the realm of AI-powered recruitment tools. These tools often utilize historical data to inform their predictions and decisions during the hiring process. If this historical data is coded with existing societal biases, such as those related to gender or race, the AI system may perpetuate these biases. For instance, it might favor certain candidates over others. This will lead to discriminatory hiring practices.

Ethical guidelines at the coding level and implementation level provides a framework to ensure AI is used responsibly, respecting human rights and promoting fairness.

The need for ethics in AI is clear and pressing. For small business owners, this means understanding the potential implications of AI systems, adopting ethical guidelines to ensure their responsible use, and being transparent about these practices with customers and stakeholders. By doing so, businesses can not only avoid potential harm and legal issues but also build trust with customers and gain a competitive edge.

OVERVIEW OF ETHICAL AI USE

AI ethics is an extension of your company values because it requires businesses to take responsibility for developing, implementing, and using their AI systems. Companies should ensure their AI systems reflect their ethical principles—from data collection and security to system monitoring and evaluation. Ethical AI use enables companies to build trust with customers, ensuring the security and privacy of data while at the same time maximizing the potential impact of their technology.

In order for small business owners to ensure their AI systems are designed and implemented ethically, they need to integrate a number of important principles into their process. Here are some action steps:

1. Understand the Basics of AI

Small business owners need to understand what AI is and how it works. This will help them to make informed decisions about AI implementation, use, and management.

2. Define Ethical Principles

Define the ethical principles that are most important to you and your business. These may include transparency (being open about how AI is being used), accountability (taking responsibility for AI outcomes), fairness (ensuring AI doesn't favor one group over another), and non-discrimination (making sure AI doesn't unjustly impact individuals based on attributes like race, gender, etc.).

3. Involve Stakeholders

Involve all relevant stakeholders—from your employees to your customers—in the discussion about AI ethics. Their input can be invaluable in understanding different perspectives and potential concerns. Showing stakeholders that you're listening to their concerns is one of the best ways to build trust with them.

4. Incorporate Ethics in AI Development Process

If you're developing AI systems in-house, ensure that your development team understands and integrates your defined ethical principles in the development process. If you're using third-party AI solutions, choose providers who prioritize ethical AI design and use.

5. Review and Test for Bias

AI systems can unintentionally perpetuate and amplify societal biases present in their training data. Regularly review and test your AI systems to identify and correct any bias. This is an ongoing process, not a one-time task.

6. Transparent Communication

Be transparent with your employees and customers about how you're using AI and how you're ensuring it's being used ethically. This will help build trust and mitigate concerns.

7. Plan for Accountability

Develop a plan to hold your business accountable for the outcomes of your AI systems. This includes having procedures in place to address and correct any issues or harmful impacts that may arise from your use of AI.

8. Ongoing Monitoring and Adjustment

Ethics in AI is not a set-and-forget principle. Continuously monitor the performance and impact of your AI systems and make adjustments as needed to uphold your ethical principles. Companies must monitor new regulations and keep up-to-date with potential changes that may affect their operations. With this in mind, businesses can proactively comply with applicable legislation while reaping the benefits of utilizing ethical AI technologies.

9. Education and Training

Provide training for your employees about the ethical use of AI. Make sure they understand why it's important and how to ensure the tools they use are aligned with your business's ethical standards.

By taking these action steps, small business owners can ensure that they're implementing and using AI in a way that aligns with ethical principles, helping to create a positive impact for their businesses, employees, and customers. The following chapter will build on this foundation, outlining the Ten Commandments of ethical AI use.

CONCLUSION

The ethics of a business serve as the invisible glue that holds the fabric of relationships together—whether they're with colleagues, other businesses, or customers. Ethics is what enables trust to flourish, building bridges of integrity that strengthen these connections.

Developing a reputation for acting ethically - or unethically - will establish the lens through which people - customers, staff, regulators - see your actions when you inevitably make a mistake.

Businesses are not known as bastions of ethics and values. The business community is notoriously viewed as taking full advantage of regulatory gaps and exploiting loopholes to maximize profits. But we do have rules in place, laws that govern society, that provide boundaries in which businesses can operate. AI is moving faster than the laws can keep up with. In the AI playground, the rules aren't clearly drawn yet. It's like the wild west where the line between the lawful and the lawless has yet to be defined.

Here's where you, as a business, have a golden opportunity. This isn't about stretching the rules to their limits—it's about drawing the line yourself and setting the standard for ethical AI usage.

Choosing to act ethically in the world of AI isn't just a path of self-protection against future laws. It's about seizing the chance to be the hero in the AI story. It's about safeguarding the public's trust in your business and ensuring you aren't part of the group that has to be reined in when regulations become standardized regarding AI.

It's about realizing that with AI, you have the power to spin the future. But with this power comes the responsibility to decide not just what we can do but what we should do. It's our responsibility to ensure that

AI doesn't just serve the business but also serves society, respects individual rights, and promotes fairness and transparency.

Stepping into the AI frontier with ethics as your guide is about more than just future-proofing your business. It's about being a trailblazer, setting the path for an AI future that aligns with our collective values. It's about shaping a future where AI isn't feared but embraced as a tool for positive change. By championing ethical AI, you're not just running a business; you're part of a revolution in the world.

---

1. The principle of "doing no harm," also known as non-maleficence, is often attributed to the Hippocratic Oath, a historic text attributed to Hippocrates, who is often regarded as the father of medicine. The Hippocratic Oath is considered one of the earliest documents that establish a framework for medical ethics.

12 NAVIGATING YOUR POLICY DECISIONS

n the heart of every successful business lies a foundation of values, principles, and ethics. Our ethics and values are usually so deep within us that we don't realize that they're driving us throughout the day. However, they're not so deep inside of us that we can't bring them in front of our faces and give them a full examination.

AI, with its transformative potential, also brings forth a slew of ethical and operational dilemmas. For small businesses, the task is twofold: understanding AI's capabilities and weaving those capabilities into the fabric of their organizational ethos.

Before any small business owner integrates AI into their operations, it is vital to embark on a journey of soul-searching. It's not just about adopting technology for efficiency's sake; it's about asking, "How does this align with who we are and what we stand for?"

SOME QUESTIONS FOR CONSIDERATION

Here are some questions to work through in the quietness of your own heart or with your team. They are essential to figure out because you want to avoid being random or a firefighter who's always addressing problems that come from messing up.

- What are the core principles and values we want to uphold in our AI development and usage?
- How will we provide oversight and governance for AI systems? Who will be involved?
- How will we evaluate, mitigate, and monitor risks from AI?
- How will we ensure responsible and ethical data collection and usage?
- How will we assess and prevent bias, discrimination, and unfair outcomes?
- How will we protect user privacy and secure sensitive data?
- How transparent will we be about our AI capabilities and usage?
- What do we need to do in order to comply with relevant laws and regulations for AI?
- How will we communicate AI use cases and get consent from customers/users?
- How will we educate our staff on responsible and ethical AI development?
- What are our protocols for auditing AI systems and updating policies?
- How will we investigate AI failures or misuse and remedy issues?
- How will we evaluate, approve, and adopt new AI technologies?
- What special considerations do we need for public-facing vs. internal AI?
- Who will be accountable and responsible for compliant AI practices?

NOW MAKE YOUR OWN TEN COMMANDMENTS

The Ten Commandments of ethical AI use in your business can serve as a clear, simple guide to working through the complex realm of artificial intelligence. These commandments are principles that establish a moral framework for AI implementation, ensuring it aligns with your company's values and ethics.

Your AI commandments set the standards for AI use in your business. They guide decision-making and shape behavior. By making these principles clear, businesses can strive to prevent the misuse of AI, ensure fair and unbiased AI decisions, and prioritize respect for human rights.

They make it clear what your business stands for when it comes to AI, giving everyone, from the top executives to the newest hires, a concrete understanding of what's acceptable and what isn't.

These commandments can apply to topics such as data privacy, transparency, non-discrimination, accountability, and much more.

Having a set of AI commandments isn't just about ticking a box; it's about creating an AI culture rooted in ethical behavior. It brings everyone on the same page, promotes a shared understanding, and serves as a reminder of the company's commitment to ethical AI use. As the world of AI continues to grow and evolve, so will the ethical challenges.

The following are the Ten Commandments of ethical AI use that every business owner should consider:

1. **Transparency**: We will ensure our AI systems operate in a manner that is transparent and understandable to our users and stakeholders.
2. **Fairness**: We will strive to eliminate bias in our AI systems and ensure they treat all individuals and groups fairly.
3. **Accountability**: We will hold ourselves accountable for our AI systems' impacts and ensure there are mechanisms in place to audit their performance and rectify any adverse outcomes.
4. **Privacy**: We will respect the privacy of our users and ensure that our AI systems handle data in a manner that safeguards personal information.

5. **Seek The Good**: We will design and use AI systems with the primary intent of benefitting users, society, and the environment.

6. **Do No Harm**: We will commit to preventing harm to individuals, society, and the environment through our AI systems.

7. **Autonomy**: We will respect human autonomy, ensuring our AI systems do not unduly influence or coerce individuals into decisions they would not otherwise make.

8. **Justice**: We will ensure our AI systems promote social justice, helping to reduce rather than exacerbate societal inequalities.

9. **Trustworthiness**: We will strive to build trust in our AI systems, demonstrating reliability and consistency in their performance and outcomes.

10. **Continuous Learning**: We will regularly review and update these commandments, reflecting changes in society, technology, and our understanding of AI's impacts.

These commandments can serve as the foundation for an ethical AI program within a business, offering a clear and robust framework for decision-making. They underscore a commitment to harnessing the power of AI responsibly, with a focus on promoting the well-being of all stakeholders and society at large.

Trying to figure out your views on AI ethics can be overwhelming. This is especially true for small business owners who are just starting to explore its potential. The transformative power of AI is undeniable, offering promising avenues to get more done, elevate processes and improve customer experiences. However, it also comes with its set of ethical challenges that cannot be overlooked. For the budding business owner, it's essential to approach AI not just as a tool but as a responsibility.

We've talked about the importance of developing your own ethics. Embrace ethics not as a hindrance but as a guiding light, ensuring that your business not only thrives in this AI era but also stands as a model of trust and integrity. It's not just about harnessing AI's capabilities; it's about doing so with a conscience.

In the following chapter, we'll look at examples of companies not following these guidelines and the risks that all businesses take when they try to take advantage of the current lack of laws surrounding AI use.

13 RISKS AND TRANSPARENCY

STRAVA'S HEATMAP HICCUP

Mark Zuckerberg is not the only Harvard alum to find himself in the controversial waters of AI ethics. Harvard classmates Mark Gainey and Michael Horvath, who founded Strava, have also encountered similar challenges. Strava gained popularity as a social network for athletes, offering a platform for users to log, analyze, and share their workouts. It particularly struck a chord with cyclists and runners.

While I have not seen its codebase, Strava uses machine learning to enhance its user experience.

Machine learning would offer personalized training suggestions based on individual activity data, update segment leaderboards in real-time, suggest popular routes derived from aggregated user paths, and personalize advertising content or promotional offers. Strava could also leverage AI for sophisticated data visualization, like the heatmap feature, and anomaly detection to ensure accurate user activity feedback.

However, in 2017, the founders' ambition led to a significant misstep.

They launched an elaborate heatmap displaying activities from users worldwide, aiming to depict popular workout routes. But an unforeseen consequence arose: it unintentionally exposed intricate activity patterns around military bases and sensitive locations. Nathan Ruser, a vigilant student, pointed out this significant security lapse. This heatmap, revealing hidden military installations and patrol routes, posed potential risks of strategic exploitation by adversaries. Strava, in damage-control mode, emphasized the anonymity of the data while pledging collaboration with military entities to address concerns.

Reacting promptly, the U.S. Department of Defense accentuated operational security and revisited policies concerning gadget usage by military personnel. The episode reminded tech innovators of the intricate responsibilities accompanying vast data dissemination.

Thankfully, all was not lost. After the 2017 heatmap incident, Strava swiftly took measures to address the security implications, underscoring that the data was anonymous and urging military users to adjust their privacy settings. In response to the concerns, the platform enhanced its privacy options, collaborated with military and governmental bodies, and introduced new app features emphasizing community and competition.

Despite the setback, Strava's growth trajectory remained robust. Co-founders Mark Gainey and Michael Horvath continued their pivotal roles, with Horvath returning as CEO in 2020. The company's proactive response and subsequent emphasis on data privacy and security helped mitigate the reputational fallout, solidifying Strava's standing as a global fitness tracking tool for athletes.

WHAT WE CAN LEARN

The Cambridge Analytica incident showcased the dangers of misusing personal data for political gain, while the Strava heatmap revealed unintended security risks in everyday fitness tracking. Both incidents highlight how even well-intended technology can have unforeseen consequences regarding our data.

Together, these stories serve as compelling reminders of the dual-edged nature of technology; they underscore how innovations aiming to foster connection and wellness can inadvertently jeopardize personal privacy and security.

As we explore how to use AI as business leaders, these stories remind us of the importance of working with care and awareness.

ADOPTING AN ETHICAL AI MINDSET WHEN INTRODUCING AI INTO YOUR BUSINESS

Ethical AI usage encourages businesses to focus on building customer trust and privacy, allowing for smoother operations and improved user experiences. It provides greater transparency and accountability in the technology's development, implementation, and usage, which helps ensure the system is used safely and securely.

This helps small businesses reduce potential risks while at the same time improving their operations by providing timely services with minimal disruption. As such, adopting ethical practices is not only beneficial to customers but also helps create a positive brand image for small businesses.

Legal frameworks are being established worldwide, and non-compliance may result in severe penalties. Beyond the legal realm, unethical AI practices can erode customer trust, dampen employee morale, place businesses at a competitive disadvantage, and lead to flawed decision-making. Ultimately, these oversights can result in significant financial losses. To foster a beneficial relationship with both customers and employees and gain a competitive edge, businesses must prioritize ethical AI practices from the outset.

TRANSPARENCY IS ALWAYS BETTER

I believe companies should be transparent with their customers about the use of AI in their customer service operations. It is important to explain why and how AI is being employed so that customers understand what services are being provided to them, as well as any potential risks associated with the use of AI technology.

Companies must ensure that customer data is kept confidential and secure at all times. This includes securely storing data, encrypting transmissions, and monitoring access to such information. Assuring customers that their personal data will not be misused or sold by the company helps build trust between the company and the customer.

Lastly, companies should empower customers by giving them the choice to opt in or out of AI-based services such as automated chatbots or intelligent analytics solutions. Providing this option for customers shows that the company respects their privacy and autonomy–a sign of a committed business partner who cares about creating a positive customer experience.

THERE'S A LOT AT STAKE

Much more must be said about the ethics of AI. Entire dissertations have been written about it. More are coming, no doubt. Right now, some of the brightest minds in the world are tackling the ethical challenges that lie ahead.

Ethics is important. Without ethics in AI, your business and our society will fail. There's a lot at stake here.

Without a proper understanding of the importance of ethical AI use, organizations may be in danger of violating regulations or losing customers' trust. Thus, businesses must incorporate ethical considerations into all AI operations to maintain customer trust and demonstrate a commitment to responsible innovation.

By doing so, small businesses are more likely to successfully implement their AI system while establishing trust and confidence in those affected by its usage.

14 HOW I WROTE A BOOK WITH THE HELP OF AI

15 EMBRACING ETHICAL WRITING IN THE AGE OF AI

I t's the age-old dream of business owners everywhere – writing a book. It's often the aspirational project that never sees the light of day due to time constraints. Let's be honest, the business hustle doesn't always allow for the quiet contemplation needed to pen an entire manuscript.

We've all heard the whispers: ghostwriting is a well-accepted practice in the literary world. But now, you don't have to hire a ghostwriter; you have AI. After all, can we genuinely believe that Phil Knight had the time to meticulously craft every word of "Shoe Dog" while managing a global empire?

But today, with the synergy of ethics and technology, you have a chance to capture your thoughts and write like never before. Take advantage of the golden age of writing and innovation, where AI can be your co-author.

THE ETHICS OF AI-ASSISTED WRITING

The use of AI, particularly in fields that have been traditionally reliant on human expertise, such as literature, often triggers debates about its ethical implications. When considering writing a book using AI, there are several perspectives to consider.

1. Authorial Intent and Authenticity

At its heart, the act of writing is about expressing thoughts, experiences, and insights. An author uses AI tools as just that – tools. Much like a painter might use a new kind of brush or a musician might incorporate a synthesizer into their composition, an AI can be a medium for the author's genuine intent. I believe that if writing is going to continue to be worth reading, the original thought, the desire to convey a message or a story, should still originate from a human.

2. Transparency

Ethical concerns often stem from the misrepresentation of AI-assisted work as purely human-derived. If authors are open about the use of AI in their writing process, they maintain transparency and honesty with their readers. When authors acknowledge the contributions of others, whether human or AI, they stay true to the ethical standards we have come to expect of published authors.

3. Democratization of Knowledge and Creativity

AI can make the act of writing more accessible. Not everyone has the privilege of formal writing training or the time to devote to lengthy research. AI tools can democratize this process, allowing more voices to be heard. Ethically, this broadening of the literary landscape can be seen as a leveling of the playing field, providing opportunities to those who might have been excluded from traditional publishing avenues.

4. Quality Control

AI tools can enhance the quality of writing by providing grammar checks, suggesting better phrasing, or offering insights that a writer might have missed. This doesn't dilute the essence of the content but rather polishes it, much like an editor would.

5. Learning and Growth

For many, writing is as much about the journey as the end product. Engaging with AI can be a dynamic learning process for the writer, helping them understand different perspectives and improving their crafts.

6. Economic and Time Efficiency

Writing is a time-consuming process, often requiring extensive research, multiple drafts, and revisions. AI can streamline these processes, making it feasible for individuals, especially professionals like business owners, to write while managing their regular responsibilities.

The ethical use of AI in writing hinges on intention, transparency, and acknowledgment. When AI becomes a collaborator rather than a crutch, when its use is transparently communicated, and when the primary intent remains the genuine conveyance of a human message or story.

The journey of putting this book together was an exciting work of learning, experimenting, and growing. It was made exponentially more manageable and more refined with ChatGPT as my super assistant.

Here is a step-by-step overview of how I utilized ChatGPT in various stages of the book's creation:

Step 1: Strategy Formation

I initiated the process with strategy formulation, where ChatGPT played a critical role in shaping the framework and approach of the book. It assisted in outlining the main ideas, themes, and overall structure, ensuring coherence and alignment with the book's objectives.

Step 2: Clarifying Thoughts

Once the strategy was set, ChatGPT acted as a sounding board, helping me articulate and refine my thoughts, ideas, and concepts. It took my rough and scattered thoughts and transformed them into clear, coherent, and concise articulations, adding depth and precision to the content.

Step 3: Grammar Checking and Refinement

Grammar and language refinement were another area where ChatGPT showcased its utility. It diligently scanned the text, ensuring grammatical accuracy, language consistency, and refinement, enhancing the readability and professionalism of the book.

Step 4: Translating Notes into Prose

ChatGPT was indispensable in converting my assorted notes and ideas into polished prose. It interpreted and weaved my notes into well-structured, flowing, and comprehensive sections, maintaining the essence and nuance of the intended message.

Step 5: Citation and Source Verification

Finding credible sources and proper citation was made hassle-free with ChatGPT. It assisted in locating relevant studies, verifying their credibility, and creating accurate citations, thus fortifying the book's content with validated information and maintaining academic integrity.

Step 6: Content Enhancement

ChatGPT's prowess in rewriting and enhancing sections of the book was invaluable. It revisited and refined various sections, optimizing content quality, ensuring clarity, and improving the overall impact and conveyance of the book's message.

Step 7: Final Review and Refinement

In the final stages, ChatGPT meticulously reviewed the entire manuscript, fine-tuning every detail, ensuring consistency, coherence, and optimal quality, preparing the book for its journey into the readers' hands.

AN AMAZING, UNPRECEDENTED GIFT TO WRITERS

The assistance of ChatGPT was an immense gift throughout this writing journey. Its multifaceted capabilities facilitated a seamless, enriched, and refined writing process, acting not just as a tool but as a collaborative companion, making the daunting task of book writing more accessible and enjoyable.

For writers seeking a symbiotic relationship with technology to enhance their creative process, ChatGPT stands as a testament to the incredible possibilities and the gift it brings to the world of writing.

I'm profoundly thankful for ChatGPT, and I'm excited for other writers to experience the empowerment and ease it brings to the writing process, helping to bring ideas to life with clarity, precision, and grace.

GO FORTH AND WRITE

Each of us carries a unique perspective, a treasure trove of experiences, and lessons that can inspire, heal, challenge, or simply entertain others.

Writing a book is not just an act of putting words on paper; it's an act of bravery, a commitment to share a piece of yourself with the world. Let not the fears of imperfection or judgment deter you.

Remember, every great author once started with a blank page and a kernel of an idea. The journey of writing can be transformative, not just for your readers but for you as well. So, seize the pen, the keyboard, or whatever tool you prefer, and let the words flow.

Your story is waiting to be told, and the world is waiting to read it. Go forth and write that book with confidence.

CONCLUSION: JUST SCRATCHING THE SURFACE OF AI ETHICS

As we conclude our section on ethics, it's evident that there is more that needs to be said and done. The integration of AI into our world demands more than mere technological mastery; it calls for ethical vigilance.

From understanding the challenges in the evolving landscape of AI ethics to deep introspection on policy alignments, businesses and individuals are tasked with balancing innovation with responsibility. The emphasis on risks and the unwavering need for transparency are steps to ensure the protection and success of both people and businesses in an AI-dominant era.

Ultimately, this section has underlined a pivotal message: as we forge ahead in the age of AI, ethical adoption in your business isn't just a consideration—it's an imperative.

FINALE - LOOKING DOWN THE PATH WHILE STANDING AT A CROSSROADS

As we tackle the many unknowns of our AI-driven future, we must remain open to new opportunities and look for ways to safely and responsibly leverage AI's power. With AI comes the potential to create innovative solutions that can transform our lives and the world around us. We can make this uncertain future brighter by staying grounded in ethical principles and continuing to work together.

As we embrace the opportunities of an AI-driven future, let us keep our eyes open for ways to use technology in beneficial, meaningful ways. This will ensure that humanity can benefit from AI technology advancements as we move into an exciting new era.

HOW AI WILL DISRUPT THE WORLD OF COUNSELLING AND MENTAL HEALTH

Let's use a case study to think about how AI could change an industry. We will randomly choose mental health and AI – because who couldn't use some more mental health these days, right?

Now, before we go down this road, let's acknowledge something: the profound power of human connection in therapy. My life is 100X better because of therapy, and there's no denying that. But, just for a moment, let's think about how AI might complement, rather than compete with, our dear human therapists.

Think of the number of times people shy away from therapy because they can't find an available slot or the right therapist near them. That's where AI comes in: always ready, always available. No waiting lists, no geographical constraints.

Then there's the vast ocean of therapeutic research, techniques, and historical knowledge. Even the most dedicated therapist can't retain it all. But an AI? It's like having an encyclopedia of therapeutic wisdom at your fingertips, up-to-date and ready to tailor advice using the very latest in mental health research.

Do you have privacy concerns about sharing your deepest issues with a human being who is likely connected to you through some small degree of separation? I don't blame you. We've all hesitated to share something personal, fearing judgment. With an AI counselor, that worry disappears. It doesn't judge, get shocked, or gossip. It's a vault, processing your concerns without any emotional baggage.

And let's face it, we humans have our off days. We get tired, we get irritated, and sometimes, our problems might cloud our judgment. In contrast, An AI counselor remains unaffected by the ebbs and flows of life, offering consistent, unbiased support.

The aim isn't to push our human therapists out of the picture. Instead, it's to paint a larger canvas where everyone can access the mental support they need regardless of their circumstances. So, while there's no replacing the human touch, there may be room for AI to sit alongside it, ensuring that no one goes without the help they seek.

THERAPISTS, DON'T RUN FROM THIS OPPORTUNITY - RUN TO IT!

Embracing AI in a therapeutic setting is not about sidelining human expertise but harnessing the power of technology to complement and elevate the services offered. If you're a counselor or therapist running

your clinic, here's how you might approach this new wave of technological assistance:

Augmenting pre-therapy processes: Before a patient begins treatment,
AI can assist in administrative tasks such as appointment scheduling,
intake forms, and even preliminary questionnaires to assess the client's
state of mind. This streamlines processes, saving time for both clients
and therapists.

Continuous support: Consider the AI bot as an extension of your
clinic, providing clients with 24/7 support. While it won't replace the
core therapy sessions, it can offer coping techniques, relaxation exercises, or simple check-ins between appointments, ensuring clients feel
supported.

Resource repository: An AI bot can quickly recommend reading materials, meditation guides, or exercises tailored to a patient's specific
issues, curated from a vast database.

Monitoring progress: AI can help track a patient's mood or stress
levels over time, offering tangible data to supplement a therapist's
qualitative assessment. This data can be invaluable in understanding
patterns, triggers, and the effectiveness of interventions.

Training and skill development: Use AI-driven platforms for your
continuous learning. These platforms can help you stay updated with
the latest research, techniques, and case studies.

Anonymity for stigma-related issues: An AI bot provides an anonymous first step for individuals reluctant to seek therapy due to societal
stigma. After initial interactions, the bot can emphasize the importance
of human-led treatment and act as a bridge to connect the individual to
a therapist.

Cultural and linguistic flexibility: AI can communicate in
multiple languages and can be programmed to be sensitive to
cultural nuances, making therapy more accessible to diverse popu-
lations.

Collaborative effort: Instead of seeing AI as a competitor, view it as a colleague. Regularly review the insights and data it provides to shape subsequent human-led therapy sessions.

Ethical and confidential use: Make sure that the AI tools you utilize prioritize client confidentiality. Ethical use of AI will boost your clinic's credibility and ensure trustworthiness in the eyes of your clients.

Educate and inform: Hold informational sessions or workshops for your clients explaining how AI complements therapy. This demystifies the technology and highlights its benefits, making clients more receptive.

By embracing AI in a therapeutic context, you're signaling to your clients that you're committed to providing the best possible care, utilizing every tool at your disposal. It's about enhancing the human touch with technological precision, ensuring that therapy is more accessible, consistent, and tailored to individual needs.

THE SAME GOES FOR ALL OF US

For all business owners figuring out the ever-evolving landscape of AI, remember this: Every technological revolution in history, from the printing press to the Internet, has been met with apprehension. However, those who embraced change and found a way to meld it with the unique value only humans can offer survived and thrived.

AI, at its heart, is a tool, not a replacement. Any machine cannot fully replicate the nuances, empathy, creativity, and complex decision-making humans bring. AI offers the ability to handle repetitive tasks, analyze vast amounts of data quickly, and even spot trends or insights that might be challenging for a human to discern. But the human touch gives these insights context, meaning, and actionable strategies.

As a business owner, here are some empowering ideas to consider:

Educate yourself: Take the time to understand AI and its potential impacts on your industry. Knowledge dispels fear, and the more you know, the better you strategize.

Human + machine synergy: Think of AI as a collaborator or a super assistant for you. Where can it handle tasks to free up more of your team's time for value-added activities?

Adaptability: Stay agile. The world of AI is continually evolving. As you experiment with AI tools, be ready to adjust your strategies based on outcomes and feedback.

Community engagement: Engage a community that is curious like you about AI. Share experiences, strategies, and insights. Collaborative thinking often leads to innovative solutions.

Ethics and trust: Trust is paramount in an age of digital transformation. Ensure any AI integration is done ethically, prioritizing customer data privacy and transparency.

Continuous learning: Encourage a culture of lifelong learning within your organization. This helps keep up with technological advancements and fosters innovation and adaptability.

Remember, business has always been about solving problems and adding value. Technology, be it AI or any other, is just another tool in your toolkit. It's the heart, the passion, the mission, and the vision of your business that truly defines its success. Embrace the future, but root your business in the timeless principles that have always made enterprises thrive: authenticity, value, and human connection.

WE SHOULD EMBRACE UNCERTAINTY IN AN AI-DRIVEN FUTURE

Indeed, the future can often be unpredictable, and many challenges are associated with transitioning to a world powered by AI technology.

However, with collaboration and a unified focus on progress and innovation, we can face these obstacles together and look forward to a brighter tomorrow.

Using our collective creativity, knowledge, and resources, we can solve complex challenges and become more productive daily. As we strive for an AI-driven future of growth and prosperity, let us always remember the importance of coming together as one collective to make this dream a reality.

HARNESSING THE NEW FRONTIER: A LESSON FROM BILLIONAIRE BEZOS

Picture this: the early 90s, a time of dial-up connections and the nascent buzz about the "Internet." Jeff Bezos, a visionary with an audacious idea, was laying the groundwork for a venture from his garage. This venture, named "Amazon," promised an expansive digital marketplace.

As he passionately shared his vision of an online retail behemoth with those around him, the response was often met with puzzled looks. The primary question echoing was, "Jeff, what's the Internet?"

Fast forward to today, where we stand on the cusp of another technological revolution: AI. Much like the Internet in its early days, AI remains enigmatic to many. Yet, its potential is colossal, akin to the boundless opportunities the Internet presented nearly three decades ago.

Our mission might not mirror the enormous scale of Bezos' ambition, but it's powered by a similar drive to innovate, expand, and touch lives. When we articulate our goal to amplify our reach using cutting-edge digital avenues, the bewilderment we often encounter mirrors Bezos' early experiences.

But herein lies the magic: just as Bezos seized the untapped potential of the Internet before it became ubiquitous, we can leverage the power of AI, setting our trajectory ahead of the curve.

Let's take a page out of history and learn from it. There will always be skeptics and late adopters. But the visionaries brave the unknown with courage and shape the future. Bezos didn't relent in the face of doubt, nor should we.

WE'VE BEEN HERE BEFORE

When elevators were first introduced, they were a marvel of technology, promising to transport people vertically without needing stairs. But, as with any new technology, there was skepticism and fear. A human attendant operated elevators to calm these fears and provide a sense of security. This attendant managed the elevator's operations and offered a reassuring presence to passengers. Over time, as people became more accustomed to the technology and its safety features, the need for an attendant diminished, and the elevator became a self-operated, integral part of modern buildings.[1]

Fast forward to today, and we see a similar pattern with driverless cars. While the technology is advanced, there's still a level of apprehension among the public. To address this, manufacturers have incorporated features that give passengers a sense of control and safety. Whether it's a steering wheel that's present but not necessary or the ability to take over the car's operations in an emergency, these features are reminiscent of the elevator attendant of the past. They're there to provide comfort and assurance as we transition to a new way of doing things.[2]

As we stand on the cusp of a new era where robots and AI become more integrated into our daily lives, it's essential to remember that this integration will be gradual. Just as we didn't jump from stairs to unattended elevators overnight, we will only leap from human-driven cars to fully autonomous vehicles with intermediate steps. As we move along with more sophisticated and helpful forms of AI, we will learn to work alongside robots, learning from them and teaching them in return. Those who embrace this change and adapt today will undoubtedly be better positioned for the future. After all, the future belongs to those who prepare for it today.

LOOKING AHEAD TO THE NEXT 20 YEARS

I really want to try to tell you about what the future is going to look like. I could try but it's too tough to say. Yogi Berra is credited with the saying, "It's tough to make predictions, especially about the future."

I'm not a futurist. I'm a realist. I know the future comes one day at a time. Today is the only day in our control.

it's crucial to approach advancements like AI with both optimism and caution. As we integrate AI into various facets of our lives, it's important to remember that, like all technological breakthroughs, it comes with its share of challenges and opportunities.

AI, in its current form, offers remarkable benefits. I've personally experienced its transformative power – it has made me more efficient, effective, and creatively liberated than ever before. AI tools have the potential to streamline our workflows, unlock new avenues of creativity, and elevate our capacity to innovate. In many ways, AI acts as a catalyst for human flourishing, pushing the boundaries of what we can achieve.

Because of AI, more people will be helped, informed, and empowered.

However, as we look towards the horizon and the prospect of Artificial General Intelligence (AGI), the picture becomes more complex. AGI, with its potential to match or surpass human intelligence, raises profound questions about the future of our society, economy, and ethics. While I am bullish on the benefits of current AI applications, I am also mindful of the potential repercussions that unchecked or poorly guided AGI development could bring.

This is where the role of our global and local leaders becomes pivotal. Just as with any powerful technology, from nuclear energy to social media, the governance of AI and AGI must be approached with wisdom, foresight, and a commitment to the greater good. We rely on democratically elected leaders, visionary policymakers, and responsible tech developers to steer this technology in a direction that benefits humanity as a whole.

As citizens, our role is to stay informed, engaged, and vigilant. We must advocate for and support leaders who prioritize ethical considerations and human well-being in the face of rapid technological change. The task at hand is not just to keep 'the bad guys' at bay, but to actively shape a future where technology, in all its forms, contributes to human flourishing.

In sum, while I embrace AI for the incredible tool it is today, enhancing my efficiency and creativity, I also recognize the need for thoughtful stewardship as we venture into the era of AGI. It's a journey of unprecedented potential, and it's up to all of us to ensure that this potential is harnessed for the good of all. The future of AI should not be a tale of unchecked technological growth, but a story of human advancement in harmony with the tools we create.

WE HAVE A LOT TO LEARN

AI is like an exciting new friend we're still getting to know. Will it be the sidekick that makes us look good, the star of the show, or the villain who betrays us and wrecks everything? Without a time-traveling device, it's tough to know. It's a wild west out there today, and while we might have some ideas, the truth is, we're all still figuring it out.

Looking ahead to the next 10 to 20 years, it's clear that AI will be playing an increasingly important role in small businesses.

Automation capabilities will become more powerful, allowing businesses to make decisions in a fraction of the time they currently require. Data analysis will become even more sophisticated, utilizing real-time data to power predictive models and anticipate customer needs. Natural language processing, text analytics, and conversational user interfaces (e.g., chatbots) will become commonplace, providing personalized customer experiences tailored to each user.

This new level of sophistication in AI technology will have far-reaching effects on small business operations—from product design and manufacturing to marketing and sales—and help them stay competitive against large corporations.

With the right investments in research and development, staff training, and legal understanding, small businesses can use AI tools to achieve their goals more efficiently and accurately than ever before.

WHAT WILL YOU DECIDE?

As the pages of this book draw to a close, the small business owner's journey is just beginning, especially at the critical intersection with artificial intelligence.

The road ahead presents three distinct choices:

1. Preserve the Status Quo

By choosing inaction, there's a looming shadow of becoming obsolete in a world where competitors, armed with AI, race ahead with speed and precision.

There's a familiarity with the current processes, and you'd avoid the initial investment that comes with new technologies. By sidestepping innovation, you risk becoming a relic of the past. In the ever-accelerating business world, competitors leveraging AI will outpace you, potentially resulting in the loss of customers and market share.

2. The Wait-and-See Stance

Going "all in-all at once" is not for everyone. There is a "second mover" advantage as long as a move is made. The cautious route may feel like the middle ground, but in a fast moving world of AI, it can quickly become a game of catch-up. If you are cautious, I know why. I don't want you to miss the opportunities captured by the early adopters. There are positives to proceeding with caution. You will feel safeguarded from the initial hiccups of AI adoption. By observing others, you can learn from their mistakes.

But you will still need to play catch up as early adopters would have established a solid AI-driven presence. This could push you further down the competition ladder. The second mover must move at some point.

3. Embrace AI's Potential

The path illuminated by this book beckons you towards harnessing AI's power right away. Embarking on this journey will refine your operations and solidify your footing in an ever-competitive, innovation-driven marketplace. By choosing this proactive path, you're placing your business at the forefront of innovation. AI can enhance efficiency, customer engagement, and business insights, ensuring you're not just keeping up but often staying ahead of the curve. Following the strategies outlined in this book makes the transition smoother, ensuring a calculated, structured, and efficient integration of AI into your business model. There's an initial learning curve and investment. However, given the exponential advantages AI offers, this is dwarfed by the benefits that can follow.

The choices you make today are not just about staying relevant but about pioneering the future. With AI as your ally, the horizons of possibilities expand. Embrace it, harness it, and let your business shine brightly in the constellation of tomorrow's market.

As you move forward, remember that today's choices shape tomorrow's success stories. The future is AI-empowered; the question is, how will your business continue to be a part of it?

---

1. Prisco, J. (2019, February 9). A short history of the elevator. CNN. https://www.cnn.com/style/article/short-history-of-the-elevator/index.html
2. LaFrance, A. (2015, December). Driverless Cars Are Like Elevators: Just another magic box with buttons in it. The Atlantic. https://www.theatlantic.com/technology/archive/2015/12/magic-boxes-with-buttons/419841/

ABOUT JON MORRISON

Jon Morrison understands the collision of confusion about AI and its unlimited potential for good.

Jon is an alumnus of Trinity Western University with an MBA, and a holder of a MA at the intersection of Philosophy and Science from Biola University, leads Get Clear with a focus on the responsible use of Artificial Intelligence (AI) in business. His academic background, enriched by his time at Oxford University, informs his approach to integrating AI into small business strategies.

Living in Abbotsford, BC, with his wife and three daughters, Jon blends his family life with his professional commitment to ethical AI applications.

At Get Clear, he spearheads initiatives aimed at empowering small businesses through AI tools that are effective yet ethically grounded.

Jon recognizes the transformative potential of AI for businesses of all sizes, emphasizing its capacity to enhance decision-making, streamline operations, and offer new marketing avenues.

Jon's approach to AI is tempered by a deep understanding of its ethical dimensions.

He advocates for the use of AI in a manner that is not only innovative but also responsible, ensuring that technological advancements align with the broader good of society. Jon and his team at Get Clear are dedicated to providing AI solutions that are accessible to small businesses, enabling them to harness technology that was once the preserve of larger corporations.

Jon's vision is to democratize access to AI, helping smaller enterprises compete on a level playing field. He believes in AI's ability to significantly boost business efficiency and revenue while maintaining ethical integrity. For Jon, the true measure of success lies in supporting small businesses to thrive in an era increasingly defined by AI.

In Jon's perspective,

> **"Our goal at Get Clear is to aid small businesses in their growth journey, utilizing AI as a tool for success, but always within an ethical and sustainable framework."**

With a commitment to ethical practices and a belief in the power of AI, Jon Morrison and his team at Get Clear are dedicated to assisting businesses in leveraging AI to achieve their goals, ensuring that their journey is marked by both technological advancement and moral responsibility.

HOW TO WORK WITH JON

Jon offers four distinct avenues for individuals and businesses to benefit from his expertise in AI and marketing.

Each path is tailored to meet different needs and preferences, ensuring a versatile and comprehensive approach to leveraging AI in your business.

Workshops (Both In-Person and Online)

Jon hosts dynamic workshops designed to provide practical insights into AI applications in business. These sessions, available both in-person and online, cater to various learning styles and schedules.

Participants will engage in interactive learning experiences, gaining hands-on knowledge about integrating AI into their business strategies.

Speaking Engagements at Your Events

As a seasoned speaker, Jon brings his wealth of knowledge and experience to your events. His presentations are not just informative but also engaging, covering a range of topics from ethical AI implementation to transformative business strategies. Jon's talks are ideal for conferences, seminars, and corporate events, offering valuable insights to a wide audience.

Personal Coaching on AI

For a more personalized approach, Jon offers one-on-one coaching sessions. These sessions are ideal for business owners and professionals looking to deepen their understanding of AI and its practical application in their specific context. Jon's coaching helps clients navigate the complexities of AI in their specific context, ensuring they make informed decisions that align with their business goals.

Hiring Get Clear for AI-Powered Marketing Resources

Jon's company, Get Clear, specializes in creating AI-powered marketing resources tailored to your business needs. From websites to StoryBrand messaging, Get Clear provides helps you market your business in the digital age.

To explore these opportunities and learn how Jon Morrison and Get Clear can empower your business with AI, visit getclear.ai. Discover the path that aligns with your needs and take the first step towards transforming your business with the power of AI.

ACKNOWLEDGMENTS

It takes a village to write a book. I want to thank those who helped make this one possible.

To Hayley Morrison, your ongoing patience and support to my endless AI musings and half-baked "what do you think about this…" ideas have been so helpful. I know AI is a bit of a stretch for you but you listened anyway. Thank you for being my sounding board and for your insights.

Gavin Dew, your insightful feedback on the draft was invaluable. Your contributions truly elevated this book to a new level. Thank you for your wisdom and guidance.

Dr. Johann Roduit, for the countless conversations, the endless ideas, and the introduction to so many tools – you're a wizard in the AI world. Your genius and friendship has been such a blessing.

Jeremy Kyle, your belief in me and your encouragement to share my learnings with the world has been a tremendous source of motivation to get this book done. Thank you for being a constant friend.

Justin Chevrier, your meticulous editing has been instrumental in shaping this book. Your tireless efforts have truly brought my thoughts and words together.

Dr. William Morgan, thank you for giving me the opportunity to share my insights and for your unwavering encouragement. Your leadership in the chiropractic community is inspiring.

Joshua Lim, your incredible tool has opened my eyes to the possibilities of AI. Thank you for brandmessage.ai and for showing the practical magic of AI.

Matt Morrison and Phil Schalm, your innovative work with the Clinic Sites platform using AI is nothing short of remarkable. It's been an eye-opener to what AI can achieve. Kudos for your excellent work.

Eddie Plenert, our many walks and your encouragement to continue writing have been invaluable. Your enthusiasm for AI's potential keeps me inspired.

Garnett Zapf, David Hill and Jordan Hynd, your companionship as fellow dads and our discussions about AI have not only made me a better person but also a better father and writer. I'm grateful for your friendship and insights.

Tim Dumas, my amazing coach, thank you for helping me get clarity on what I'm supposed to be doing with my life and time.

Grant Strachan, it's been a joy to talk about AI with you. I hope you continue to leverage the opportunity to grow your practice.

I'm thankful for Brent Groen, Ian Angell and the business faculty at Trinity Western University who taught me about the intersection of AI and business during my MBA program.

Dr. Bobby Maybee, I'm grateful for the chance you gave me to present my work for the first time. Your passion for innovation and leadership is contagious and inspiring.

To the members of the FTCA. It's been a joy to serve your community. Thanks for your openness to explore how AI can help you build a faster, smarter and more efficient practice.

Finally, to those who continue to work hard and free me up to write books, I'm thankful. I'm thinking of Daniel Goertz, Joshua Redekop, and Jonathon Vogel. Your efforts and creativity are so appreciated.

Thanks to those who were willing to take the kids while I spent hours on my laptop: Daryl Goertz, Diane Goertz, and D.J. Groen. You are a gift to us all.

To my parents who modelled that being an entrepreneur is a cool and crazy way to do it - to take risks and try new things, I thank you and love you dearly.

To all the small business owners who keep our economy going, our people employed and work so hard to build a great life for their families - I acknowledge you. I hope AI can be another one of the tools you use to make your business just a little better so that our lives can be a little better.

www.ingramcontent.com/pod-product-compliance
Lightning Source LLC
Chambersburg PA
CBHW072204290526
45794CB00004B/1643

9798865671091